BREAKING DEMONIC STRONGHOLDS

DESTINY IMAGE PRODUCTS BY DON NORI SR.

Books

The Angel and the Judgment

Breaking Generational Curses

Hope of a Nation That Prays

Love Shack

Manifest Presence

The Prayer God Loves to Answer

Romancing the Divine

Secrets of the Most Holy Place, Volumes 1 & 2

Tales of Brokenness

You Can Pray in Tongues

Breaking Demonic Strongholds

VIDEO

The Dream and the Church, DVD

Freedom From Guilt, DVD

Introduction to the Most Holy Place, DVD

AUDIO

A Deeper Walk Through the Temple, CD

How to Give Yourself to His Presence, CD

Inside the Holy of Holies, CD

Walk Through the Temple, CD

AVAILABLE FROM DESTINY IMAGE PUBLISHERS

BREAKING DEMONIC STRONGHOLDS

DEFEATING THE LIES OF SATAN

DON NORI SR.

So, put yourselves under God's authority. Resist the Devil and he will run away from you (James 4:7).

DESTINY IMAGE® PUBLISHERS, INC.

P.O. Box 310, Shippensburg, PA 17257-0310

"Speaking to the Purposes of God for This Generation and for the Generations to Come."

This book and all other Destiny Image, Revival Press, MercyPlace, Fresh Bread, Destiny Image Fiction, and Treasure House books are available at Christian bookstores and distributors worldwide.

For a U.S. bookstore nearest you, **call 1-800-722-6774.**

For more information on foreign distributors, **call 717-532-3040.**

Reach us on the Internet: **www.destinyimage.com.**

ISBN 10: 0-7684-3166-2

ISBN 13: 978-0-7684-3166-7

For Worldwide Distribution, Printed in the U.S.A.

1 2 3 4 5 6 7 8 9 10 11 / 13 12 11 10

O Simon, Simon Peter. Listen! Satan has asked to sift all of you like a farmer sifts his wheat. I have prayed that you will not lose your faith! (Luke 22:31)

Our fight is not against human beings. No, it is against rulers, against authorities, against world powers of this darkness, and against evil spiritual beings in the heavenly world (Ephesians 6:12).

TABLE OF CONTENTS

Lord Jesus,

I am reading this book because I need your help to understand how to live a happy and fulfilled Christian Life, completely free from demonic harassment and the confusion that follows.

I trust you. I believe you. Please open my heart and my mind to see and understand the enemy's tricks and lies. Be with me as I read these pages and open the eyes of my understanding so I might experience the power to overcome and win the battle against the trickster.

In Your Name, I pray. Amen.

Chapter 1

REALITY 101

I studied, and I tried very hard to find wisdom. I tried to find some meaning for everything. I learned that it is stupid to do evil. And, it is crazy to act like a fool (Ecclesiastes 7:25).

Do you ever just wonder? I do. I wonder all the time. In fact, I was just wondering what I could possibility tell you about the reality of God that would immediately grab your heart and make you want to read every word of this book. It would be easier to tell you about the reality of the demonic world. It seems that nearly everyone has a mysterious need to read about the stuff of demonic manifestations. Books like that keep people reading for hours. But what about the stuff of divine manifestations? What about the daily, hourly, minute-by-minute intervention of the Lord on behalf of those who trust in His lovingkindness and care?

There are those who are too quick to acknowledge the presence and activity of our defeated, powerless, lying, deceiving, and sniveling enemy of our soul. His so-called power reminds me of the Wizard of Oz, all smoke and no real authority. All hype and no substance, all lies and no hope. In spite of this, many people are less inclined to give the Lord the same force of reality that is so easily given to satan.

Folks are far too willing to keep the enemy in our faith, but less willing to keep Jesus in our faith! There is no doubt that the hope of the Church is the builder of the Church, Jesus Christ. There is no doubt that if we are to flesh out the true victory of our risen Lord, we must ask Him to teach us the true power of the Risen Lord and the true nature of our once-and-for-all defeated enemy.

Each year you hear the phrase, "Keep Christ in Christmas!" Well, how about, "Keep Christ in Christian"?

Our greatest threat is not Islam, politicians, or Hollywood. Our greatest threat comes from those among us who either dumb down the Christian experience by eliminating the supernatural reality of the living Christ of God, or offer solutions that do not recognize the power of Him who overcame death.

If there is one thing we do not need, it is another book with the best ideas of mere mortals for overcoming the enemy of our souls. Nor do we need a book filled with the graphic details of casting out unwilling devils. We certainly do not need a theology that develops patterns of demonic behavior based on what these random spirits shout out as they are sent into the abyss.

The world is full of the wisdom of man and the doctrines of demons. Under the guise of theological treatises, we have been bombarded with stuff that is meant to help humanity understand and overcome the devil—in reality, it has had little effect on the believer's ability to lead a solid and fruitful life.

What is needed is a carefully and biblically crafted appreciation of the enemy's goals, a grasp of his determination, and a picture of his tactics. Additionally, a clear presentation of his defeat and what that defeat means, in practical terms, to those who call upon the name of our Lord Jesus Christ helps to declare his status as a defeated enemy. Without this knowledge, you will never recognize the enemy's trickery, let alone overcome it. For the voice of defeated enemy sounds arrogant, truthful, and, of course, helpful. But do not be fooled by his apparent concern for your well-being. He is bent on your destruction, even though he screams his taunts from the depths of his powerlessness.

When the former dictator of Iraq, Saddam Hussein, was on trial for war crimes, his actions were unbelievable. He shouted as though he still had authority. He made demands as though he would be obeyed and talked of his future as though he was still the leader of that country. In reality, he didn't seem to get it. He was finished. His reign of terror was over. He was defeated and powerless. His threats meant nothing, he could do nothing.

First, we must learn to discern the spirits. We must take the time to learn God's Word and discover the sense or feeling of the Spirit of the Lord. Becoming sensitive to God is one of the first and most powerful ways to begin to stand for all Jesus sealed for you when He rose from the dead. The trickery of the enemy is subtle to the natural mind, but not so evasive to the spiritually minded. Remember, I said the enemy is defeated, but he is not stupid. He knows us well, as we discover in the Book of Job. The enemy sees, hears, understands, and follows the work of the Lord in our hearts. This is his first advantage over most of us, who live by the letter of the Word rather than by the Spirit of the Lord as well as the written Word. If he can see what is going on in the spirit realm and we cannot, he has a decided advantage. His trickery will only consistently work on those who are not actively practicing His Presence and pursuing life in the Holy Spirit. It is there that our minds are renewed, and we are taught to discern the difference between the merely good and the Spirit of the Lord. For the written Word, apart from the Spirit of the Lord, is the law that kills. Just as the Scripture tells us, we are *"...able ministers of a new agreement, which is spiritual, not literal. The letter of the law kills, but the Spirit gives life"* (2 Cor. 3:6).

LIVING IN UNION

To be in union with God is to touch, experience, and live in the supernatural, the realm of all-God. Even though God dwells in every dimension, humans are body, soul, and spirit. To be aware of and live in the Spirit, we must realize that this realm exists. We must strive to give ourselves to Him that we too may experience the fullness of His intentions for us, in this realm of eternal life and supernatural fulfillment. Our five senses only put us in touch with the natural world, but our spirits put us in touch with the spirit realm. In that realm we can experience Him in a way that we never dreamed possible. In the spirit realm, the Holy Spirit pours into our spirit so that we can know the plan of God, understand our role in it, and dedicate ourselves to its fulfillment.

In the natural realm, the dimension in which we live in our bodies, our soul is fed information from the five senses. It is the task of our five natural senses to gather information from this natural realm and feed it to our soul—our mind, will, and emotions.

Your soul interprets this information and makes decisions accordingly. If you are tuned only to the five senses, you only get a portion of the information you need to make decisions. That means you will miss much vital information that can only be sensed by your spirit and delivered to your soul through that spirit. The spirit realm is just as real as the natural realm. It contains vital information as to the course and function of your life. It keeps us balanced in our overall understanding of God, the universe, and our place here on earth. If we concentrate on the input of the five senses while ignoring the input of the spirit, we become hardened to what we see from the spirit realm. We then become like a car trying to go straight ahead with one brake locked. We can only go in circles while making a lot of smoke and noise! It may look spiritual to some, but it gets us nowhere. The more naturally minded we are, the more we will be drawn to the natural realm. When this happens, the more distant and elusive the spirit realm will seem to become.

Also, the more naturally minded, or carnally minded, we become, the more the power of the flesh, along with its lusts and desires, will try to rule us. If it can't take us over, it will certainly distract us from our goal of listening and following the Lord. Remember, the enemy doesn't care if you give in to his temptation or spend your time and energy fighting him. The trickster is happy as long as you are *not* doing the will of God. So a day in which you battle temptation and squeak through without sin is still a success for the enemy, for you were focused on the temptation, and therefore did not tap in to the supernatural resources of the realm of all-God.

YOUR MOST PRECIOUS GIFT

Your soul is where your most precious gift from God rests. That gift is your free will. The information from the spirit and natural realms dukes it out in your mind. It is there that the data you have received convince you to do what you do.

Most folks do not realize the powerful significance of this. God has always had people who love Him according to their own desire. Shotgun weddings seldom work in the natural, and they rarely work in the Spirit. He gives us a choice to serve Him or not to serve Him. The data from the Spirit are vital to the decisions we make as we seek to find and serve the Lord we love. When we focus solely on either realm, we become imbalanced and do not adequately see the entire picture.

Here is the balance from the Scriptures:

> *All people who are being led by God's Spirit are sons of God* (Romans 8:14).

> *An uninspired person does not receive messages from God's Spirit. To him, they are without meaning; he cannot understand them. They can only be understood in a Spiritual way* (1 Corinthians 2:14).

The incredible thing about God is that He saw the influence the enemy would have over our bodies. He therefore decided to take up residence *within* us, placing a beachhead of His Kingdom in the midst of formerly occupied territory. Remember, we were bought by Jesus, and He owns us body, soul, and spirit. He can live, occupy, and bless wherever He wants!

> *Surely you realize that your body is a temple sanctuary? You have received the Holy Spirit from God. The Holy Spirit is inside you—in the temple sanctuary. You don't belong to yourselves* (1 Corinthians 6:19).

> *The letter of the law kills, but the Spirit gives life!* (2 Corinthians 3:6).

> *The Spirit is "the Lord." There is freedom wherever the Spirit of the Lord is* (2 Corinthians 3:17).

> *Since we get life from the Spirit, we should follow the Spirit* (Galatians 5:25).

God describes Himself as "I AM" not once or twice but 1,033 times. "I AM" describes His existence in the realm of spirit. This is a place where there is no time as we know it. This spirit realm is the place of our completion. It is where Jesus went to prepare a place for us to dwell. He prepared the realm of Spirit for us, not to occasionally visit, but permanently dwell. We are intended to dwell in, or be consciously aware of both the natural and spiritual realm. He went to prepare a place of safety in the spirit realm. We are protected from all that dwells in this realm that opposes God. It is as though we live in an impenetrable ship in deep space. We live in the Spirit, while in the spirit world.

A few Scripture examples of the spirit realm follow:

> *Since I am leaving to prepare a place for you, you can be sure that I will come back and take you with me, so that you will be where I am* (John 14:3).

[Jesus said,] *I don't come from the world; they don't come from the world, either"* (John 17:16).

Father, You loved Me before the world was created. You have given Me glory. I want them to see it. I want them to be with Me, where I will be (John 17:24).

And exactly where *is* He? He is in the dimension of spirit. He is outside of time and space. He is outside the rules of physics that govern this realm. He carried the cup of His own blood to this realm of spirit. He delivered it to the throne of God, the Mercy Seat, your heart, where He sprinkled it pure so the Father and Son could seat themselves permanently in you. He prepared a place there for your soul to rest. It is where His counsel, His compassion, His wisdom, and His mercy are available to you. It is here that He wants us to allow Him to change our minds so we can believe, receive, and experience everything He has for us.

TRUE SPIRITUALITY

What is true spirituality, and why should we want it? True spirituality is the relinquishing of our own will to the will of God. This surrender releases Him to pour His life into you and through you. It is a win-win proposition. We receive from Him for our own personal benefit as well as for the benefit of those around us. We are truly a river. His life flows out from us, nourishing and regenerating our lives first and the world around us in the process. Yes, changing the world is a natural result of the river of God's life flowing through us. We do not have to try to flow, we just flow. Just as life flourishes along a river, life flourishes around us. The hungry and thirsty are attracted to a river for a river sustains, produces and gives life, just as we do.

Many see this river of God as a cure-all for their own personal needs and problems, without regard to the benefit of the world around them, however, the heart of our destiny is understanding the nature of God's ever-expanding influence on the worlds around us. So many believers are consistently dissatisfied with their Christian experience. This unsettledness is directly related to the selfish attitude with which we approach blessing. We are healed, delivered, forgiven, and strengthened so that His life can flow through us to the world. Anything less is ultimately frustrating and unsatisfying. True spirituality is understanding that blessing is a natural, or, shall I say, supernatural result of serving Him. The blessings follow us; they do not lead us. His life flows through us. We can often see the fruit of this flow as we live our lives and allow God to live His life naturally through us.

So let Him live through you. Be content in what He has given you, knowing that the more you yield, the more you experience His supernatural power. Be happy to hear His voice and commit yourself to His purposes and see what will happen. Blessing will become a way of life.

True spirituality is also marked by the fruit of love, joy, peace, patience, gentleness, goodness, meekness, self-control, and steady faith toward God. The life of God oozes through a spiritual person. It is a liberating and fulfilling way of life, for spirituality results in understanding that God is the all-in-all in you. Your striving ceases. You discover that His burden is truly easy and His load is light. Serving God as a believer is an exhilarating lifestyle for the spiritual person, for your job is to relax, cease from your own ways, yield to Him, and let Him minister His Life in His own way in you and through you.

True spirituality is not in doctrine; it is the reality of the life that *lives* the doctrine. If a doctrine cannot be lived, it is not true, as doctrine flows from reality. Doctrine can never make reality; it either defines reality or limits it.

RAW GOSPEL

There is something about true spirituality that we have missed. There is a depth of reality, of existence that changes us completely. We no longer need to resist reality, dumb down the Gospel, or try to explain away the supernatural activity of God. God can't, won't, didn't, doesn't—are phrases that you no longer have to accept. God is infinitely bigger, wiser, and more involved with all of humanity than we can imagine. He can do and will do anything we let Him do. This is the raw Gospel. This is the truth without limitations, definitions, or boundaries. This is accepting the things of God as He does them, without resistance or fear.

We are meant to be spiritual people living in this world, this dimension, but spiritually connected and in union with God. We are in this world, but not of this world: *"I do not pray that You take them out of the world—just keep them from the evil one. I don't come from the world; they don't come from the world, either"* (John 17:15-16).

Jesus was heavenly minded *and* earthly good. True spirituality means that the more heavenly minded we are, the more earthly good we are.

True spirituality means you are connected with God. Now, what does *that* mean? It means you see as He sees. Feel what He feels. Love what He loves. It means your spirit is literally "plugged in" to His Spirit. Everything He is and has can now be in your experience.

We are created to dwell in the Spirit. Our spirit was created to be in union with God. Like a hand fits in a glove, we were made to be one with Him—now, in this life.

FULFILLED ONLY IN HIM

We are not fulfilled without Him, without connecting to Him and His reality. This is not a profound statement. Every human being knows they have an inner need. But not everyone knows how to fill that need. It is frustrating for many to discover that the things that are supposed to bring peace do not accomplish that desire. Church services, programs, rituals, and traditions may all have their place, but they cannot *replace* Him. They are very poor substitutes for His manifest Presence.

Religion, in general, tries to fill our God-sized hole. But most don't realize that somewhere along the way we have lost His Presence. Only the Presence of God will satisfy our inner yearning, and only union with Him will bring ultimate satisfaction. Nothing else works; nothing else *can* work. Our spirit cries for Him and will not be satisfied with anything less than Him.

HARMONY WITH GOD

Recognizing His Presence and becoming complete in Him is possible: *"This same Spirit agrees with our spirits, that we are God's children"* (Rom. 8:16). As we tune in to God's Spirit, our spirits will "agree" and harmonize with Him. Harmony in music is a beautiful, indescribable blending of lesser sounds that magnifies their beauty, creating a whole that is much more elegant than the individual parts. The blending voices in a choir can create an enchanting sound that no one singer could achieve. A string quartet produces a sound that makes your heart dance with its beauty. Harmony in nature is a mystery that baffles the best of our scientists. The interactions of nature and quiet interdependence of each life form is a wonder to behold.

But what is harmony with God? It is the blending of two life forces in voluntary abandonment to one another. It is the entrusting of our body, soul, and spirit to Him in the intimacy of our most secret fears and pain. It is as magnificent as love itself, as private as the marriage bed, and as mysterious and wonderful as the birth of a child. Harmony with God is where everything happens, and I do mean *everything*. Harmony, or union with God, proclaims to every dimension of existence that there is a relationship that death itself cannot destroy, a love that fear cannot confuse, and a future that the enemy cannot deny. It is the free flow of all that is God—all that is wonderful, hopeful, and fulfilling. Harmony is where life begins, and it is why life will never end. Harmony with God is the song of the night season and healing balm in times of trouble. It is the hope of tomorrow and the reason we laugh and sing and give and gather. Harmony with God, union with our Creator, is why we are born. As amazing as it sounds, this union of spirit to Spirit is coveted so much by your Lord that He gave Himself to experience this union with you alone.

This is more real than you can imagine. It is the supernatural reality of God's never-changing love for you. It is available to all who call to Him. It is available to you, for He wants you more than you can ever imagine. Even as I write this, I am frustrated by the limitation of words to express the inexpressible and to convey the essence of true spiritual reality. There is no adequate way to say it: He loves you. He wants you.

DOES GOD WANT *ME?*

Yes! Don't listen to others; listen to God. Listen to your heart! God gathers; man scatters. God forgives; man makes you feel guilty. God loves you; man judges you. God wants the best for you; man is jealous at your success. I know and understand that we are safe in the counsel of many (see Prov. 11:14). I understand that we have pastors who watch after our souls. But at the end of the day, you cannot give up the personal joy of fellowship with Him, including, but not limited to, hearing God's voice. That is a most difficult concept to live by. You, personally, are ultimately desired by your Lord. You alone bear the blessings and the consequences of responding to God. Jesus is the mediator between God and man. Jesus' resurrection and the blood of Jesus poured out on the Mercy Seat (God's Throne) give you direct communication with your God. That is how much He loves you! He wants you to fellowship directly with Him.

God *does* want you—no matter what others say, and no matter what you think of yourself. God wants you to be as close to Him as possible—living in and through Him. You can accomplish this by believing that *"there is no condemnation now for those people who are in Christ Jesus"* (Rom. 8:1).

God welcomes you to His supernatural reality because He loves you and forgives you—always and forever.

> *As high as the sky is above the earth, so great is His constant love for those who revere Him. He has taken our sins away from us, as far as the east is from the west* (Psalm 103:11-12).

> *The Always-Present One says, "Come, we will talk these things over. Your sins are red like deep red cloth. But they can be white as snow. Your sins are bright red. But you can be white like wool* (Isaiah 1:18).

All of us have sinned and fallen short of His commands. We are humans who are selfish, stubborn, and fiercely independent. Too many times we want to do things "our way" without even consulting God, as a result, when things turn out badly, He is the first one we turn to in order to have someone to complain to and to blame.

Here is a better place to live. Remember that *"He shows those who are not proud how to do right. He teaches them His way"* (Ps. 25:9). To live a life of humility is to live a life of simple submission and repentance to Him. When you live in repentance, you will hear His voice—and His voice will set you free:

> *I will instruct you. I will teach you which way to go. I will guide you and watch over you* (Psalm 32:8).

Listen to King David as he recounts his repentance before the Lord:

> *Then I admitted my sins to You. I did not hide my guilt. I thought: "I will confess my wrongs to the Always-Present One!" And, You did forgive my sins. (Selah). For this reason, let each one who is godly pray to You while they still can. When troubles rise up like a flood of huge waters, they will not reach that person. You are my Hiding Place. You protect*

me from my troubles. You surround me with songs of victory (Selah) (Psalm 32:5-7).

God is so big He can devote all His time to each one of us individually. I cannot say this enough! He is near. He hears. He understands. He cares. He loves. He is actively involved with our lives!

O One Who Is Always Present, You have examined me. You know everything there is about me. You know when I sit down and when I get up. From a distance, You understand my thoughts. You know where I go and where I lie down. You are familiar with all of my ways. O One Who Is Always Present, even before I say a word, behold, You already know what I am going to say. You surround me—in front and in back. You have put Your hand upon me. Such knowledge is too wonderful for me. It is more than I can understand (Psalm 139:1-6).

He knows our lives. He knows our strengths, our weaknesses, our fears, our joys. He knows our gifts and our personal potential because He gave each of us that potential. He has dreamed a wonderful dream for you and me that He fully intends to fulfill in this life if we will only listen to Him, respond to Him, obey Him.

We do not have to be afraid of His intentions for us. We do not have to be the kind of believer described here:

So, don't be like a horse or a donkey; they don't understand. They must be led with bits, with bridles, and with reins, or they will not come near you (Psalm 32:9).

You can be involved, immersed in, and possessed by the Holy Spirit, knowing that, in all He does, He always has your best interest in mind.

HOLINESS—NOT WHAT YOU THINK

Holiness will separate the earthly from the spiritual. The process of holiness is the process of separating the things that are of God from the things that distract us from God. There is a big difference between holiness and legalism. Holiness brings us closer to Jesus and allows us to hear His voice. Legalism is the function of the flesh and takes us away from Jesus. Legalism assumes that refraining from certain things is what God really requires, but does not bring you into relationship with God. True holiness, however, draws to God from our hearts, which naturally separates from the things of the flesh that will harm us and our friendship with God. Holiness is not in dress or actions, but in the condition of the heart.

To make ourselves available for His indwelling and our access to His supernatural reality, we need to deny the deeds of the flesh that are the attributes of humankind apart from God:

Human nature does things which are wrong. These are clear: committing sexual sin, not being pure, having orgies, worshiping false gods, practicing witchcraft, hating people, making trouble, being jealous, becoming too angry, being selfish, making people angry with each other, causing divisions, envying others, getting drunk, having wild parties, and other such things (Galatians 5:19-21).

The opposite of fleshly attributes is the fruit of the Spirit:

But the Spirit produces: love, joy, peace, patience, kindness, goodness, faithfulness, gentleness, self-control (Galatians 5:22-23).

The process of holiness is the process of separating ourselves from the things of the world, for these things cloud up the spiritual atmosphere, denying us the opportunity to experience His nearness, hear His voice, and understand His ways. Contrary to popular belief, holiness is not an end in itself. It is the means to a quiet and clear spirit that can enjoy static-free communion with God. Many things have no evil in themselves, but when they distract from my ability to experience Him, they need to go. At the end of the day, you are the only one who knows what these things might be, and you alone make the decision to lay them aside, even if for only a season, until your communion with Him is where you want it to be.

WALKING IN THE SPIRIT

What does it mean to walk in the Spirit? It simply means to respond to the Holy Spirit as a way of life. That's it.

But to achieve a walk in the Spirit requires making decisions that will make this a reality in our lives. First we need to separate ourselves from the noise of the day that overpowers the sense of His Presence. The noise I refer to is not just the noise of the flesh, which are those things that tempt us and draw us away from Him but also good things that we fill our minds with that can still drown out the voice of our Lord. Radio, even Christian radio, cannot replace the sound of His voice. In fact, even worship music, listening to a CD of a good speaker or even an audio book, can distract us. We need time to be quiet, time to listen, time to rest in Him. This is becoming harder and harder as our world is continually adding more "noise" such as cell phones, 24-hour news, sports, entertainment, and the Internet.

My own personal separation unto the Lord has become a top priority for me. Even though I have such a busy schedule, I have discovered times of solitude while driving with the radio and even Christian music sometimes turned off. The early and late evenings are special, and I covet those times of quiet meditation when His Presence is near and I allow Him to strengthen and encourage me. Even though I love Christian music, I will shut it off in lieu of listening to Him.

So I often say no to certain things like television, movies, news, the Internet, iPod, iPhone, Facebook, and others. These things and many others have the tendency to distract me unnecessarily so I can't hear the Lord's voice or experience His nearness in my life.

But I know it is not easy to simply say no to these things. I enjoy them. I need entertainment, and I need friends like anyone else. But I am jealous for my time with the Lord. It is difficult to see sometimes, but even good things can drag you down from the realm of spirit into the soulish, fleshly realm where nothing of eternal consequence happens.

I am not suggesting that we eliminate any of these things from your life. I just want you to be sure you are taking time to listen exclusively to Him, meditating on His Word and thanking Him for all He does for you.

Success is a series of right decisions. It is a series of thought-out, prayed-over choices that lead us directly into the dream God has dreamed for us. When Paul said, *"...I die daily"* (1 Cor. 15:31 NASB), he meant that he was denying himself the things that distracted him from God's plan. He was giving God first place in his life, even though it was sometimes difficult, even life-threatening. That is how convinced Paul was that God had his best interests at heart and that the purposes of God would be seen through his life. Paul suffered because he knew that as he died to himself God could use him more completely. Paul knew that the way to joy, peace, and fulfillment was tied to dying to his own will and taking up God's will.

WALKING BY THE SPIRIT IS A PROCESS TOO!

Walking by the Spirit is a process. As we continually say yes to Jesus, our stubborn human ways become weaker. We learn to obey the Lord—in fact, we learn to covet obedience to the Lord because we begin to discover the ecstasy of loving Him.

> *That's why we never give up. Even though our physical bodies are wearing out, our spirits are getting younger*

every day. The troubles we now have will last only a short time. They are working out a far greater eternal glory for us, which is worth so much more than what we are suffering now (2 Corinthians 4:16-17).

I found that my life is the fullest when I focus on Second Corinthians 4:18: *"We shouldn't look at things which can be seen. Instead, we should look for things which cannot be seen. What is seen is only temporary, but what is unseen lasts forever."* By focusing on what cannot be seen we open ourselves to God's vast supernatural reality where there are no limits to our potential, to our joy, to our communion with God.

The natural realm has its limitations. It is finite. But we are not mere mortals; we are spiritual beings and children of the Most High God. We are constructed to bring two realms together; thus, we are partakers of God's great Plan for His Kingdom. Jesus taught us to pray for it: *"This is the way you should pray: 'Father in heaven, may Your name always be kept holy. May Your kingdom come. May what You want done be done. May it always be here on earth as it is in heaven'"* (Matt. 6:9-10).

Chapter 2

BEYOND
THE FIVE SENSES

Thou wilt keep him in perfect peace, whose mind is stayed on Thee: because he trusteth in Thee (Isaiah 26:3 KJV).

Discernment does not begin with what we can touch, see, smell, hear, or taste. Recognizing the work of the Holy Spirit goes to the deepest part of who we are. We are not like so many others who depend on the five senses alone to attempt to discern the spiritual. The spiritual cannot be discerned by anything that is natural. The five senses cannot connect to another dimension. Unfortunately, many Christians have substituted the five senses for their spiritual senses, mistakenly thinking that we are capable of true discernment with the intellect alone.

The dimensions around us are full of raw data, transmitted to your soul to be sifted, refined, analyzed, and ultimately used in the decision-making process. These raw data are sent to our minds from our five senses *and* from our spirit. Information does not enter our souls already discerned. It comes as simple bits of data that we then need to interpret and discern. Our soul interprets this information and makes decisions accordingly. The typical unregenerated mind cannot understand the information it receives from the realm of spirit since this information is only appraised spiritually. Our five senses reject the things of spirit that do not compute with the things of the natural. That is why miracles are so hard to accept. The natural mind cannot accept spiritual healing, turning water into wine, speaking in tongues, or even resurrection from the dead. The mind that has been transformed by the Lord will find the miraculous much easier to accept and fellowship with the Lord much easier to enjoy. It is essential that we allow God to renew our minds in order to adequately understand and discern the information we are constantly receiving from the five senses and from our spirit.

If we are tuned in only to the five senses, we are getting just a portion of the information we need to make correct decisions. The spirit realm is just as real as the natural realm. It contains vital information as to the course and function of our lives. Our spirits *live and exist* in this dimension of spirit. When we do not hear or regard this data, our lives are shallow indeed.

True reality is not a combination of what your human body can feel, observe, smell, hear, or taste by the five senses alone. True reality is actually what is happening in the realm of the spirit and in the natural realm. The data are then processed by our soul, and we get a real picture of what is true reality. When we respond to the activity and data from these dimensions together, a clear picture of circumstances and a confident course of action emerges. If we are not aware of what is happening around us, dimensionally speaking, we are sure to fall into the trap of mistaking the desires, passions, and emotions of the spirit realm. Discernment is a gift and an art that is learned through time with Him. The key to a successful, well-rounded ability to make well-informed decisions is becoming a discerner of the spirit realm. Suffice it to say that we must submit ourselves to the hand of God in worship and meditation in the anticipation that He will train our minds to receive and discern the data from all dimensions properly.

But, you may wonder, *don't we want the feelings and desires and emotions of God to be our own?* Most certainly we do. But it is also vital that we can discern the difference between what is coming from God and what is coming from the evil one. Trickery is satan's most successful tool for turning God's children away from Him.

Turning Christians against each other is one of satan's cruelest but most surefire ways to sabotage the Church that Jesus is building. Instead of focusing on ourselves, we need to see others and their troubles through Christ Himself, through the Holy Spirit. This way, not only do we see others the way God sees them, but we can see ourselves as we truly are without Him—lost and dead—and we can pray for others with sincere compassion as we see their faults. When we understand that we have faults as well, our prayers are filled with more compassion and understanding. To be sure, slander, gossip, and idle talk cease when we see ourselves through the realm of His Spirit. These deeds of the flesh are certain signs that we have never really seen the Lord or ourselves.

LORD, GIVE ME POWER OVER THE DEVIL!

"Lord, give me power over the devil!" Great prayer, but you already have all the power over the devil that you can possibly have. When you realize that your fate is not sealed within this finite dimension of only five senses, you will soar with the eagles rather than sparring with the devil. In fact, you are stronger than the devil. It just takes awhile for you to get used to it. However, once you "get it," you will win in every way and every day.

Think about it. Wouldn't it be great to be free from the tormenting, strength-siphoning lies that ring in your mind much of the time? Wouldn't it be great not to be constantly arguing with the enemy?

Years ago I lived a life of nearly full-time harassment from the enemy. From the time I awoke in the morning until I fell asleep at night, lies filled my mind about my personal worth and what others thought about me. As this oppression increased, it began to affect me physically. I would get lost driving through the town I had lived in for many years. I was dizzy, nauseous, depressed, and confused. At the time, the physical problems seemed not to be connected with the attacks I was experiencing from the enemy. My wife, Cathy, took me to specialist after specialist. None could find a problem. It was very frustrating. But then I began wondering if my physical problems were natural manifestations of what I was suffering in the spirit. Many friends and family were praying for my healing. But the torment never ended. I began to seriously seek the Lord about the possible spiritual source of these physical problems.

One Sunday morning something incredible happened. Cathy and I were accustomed to sitting either in the first or second row for church services. This day was no different. During the time of worship, the Presence of the Lord was so real. I was still so tormented by the voices of destruction that they made it impossible for me to participate in the corporate worship experience. It was strange that in the midst of such engulfing torment I still knew and was experiencing His Presence so vividly.

As I was crying out to God for the strength to fight this battle, something extraordinary happened. The Lord said to me, "Go to Isaiah 51:22." To be completely honest, I was praying one of those desperate prayers that one does not expect to be answered. You know that kind of prayer—more of a whiny, complaining prayer about things being so bad. At any rate, I was not expecting an answer, so when this verse came into my heart, I was rather sure it was going to be my answer from the Lord. The verse reads, *"Thus says your Lord, the Lord, even your God Who contends for His people, 'Behold, I have taken out of your hand the cup of reeling; the chalice of My anger, you will never drink it again'"* (Isa. 51:22 NASB).

It was amazing. My first thought: *"God contends for me. I don't have to battle the enemy, it is **His** fight. He fights for **me**. It is not **my** battle!"* Instantly the voices stopped and have not returned these many years.

Thank God. I did not need to be delivered. I did not need to memorize a verse. I did not need to "claim it." I did not need more faith. I had to see it within my spirit. I had a revelation that I did not need to fight my own war. Jesus had fought the war and had already won it once and for all. When the revelation came into my soul, my mind was changed, and the torment ended, permanently.

Your war is over. The trickster in your life is defeated. I did not realize this, so I fought in my own strength using all the tools of the five senses. But as soon as I heard these words from the Lord Jesus, I knew that it was not my battle to wage. This is not to say that we should not do whatever we feel we must do, but when we have a clear revelation on a matter, it brings faith, peace, and most of all, results.

Stories are often told about Japanese soldiers who were left on remote islands in the South China Sea. Years after World War II was over, they were still living as though the war was being waged. Many believers live the same kind of life. They live as though the war for their souls is still going on. They continue to struggle with the torment and the possibility of instant attack and death! This way of living opens the door for the enemy of our souls who is defeated but has never signed an armistice. He lives and acts and lies as though he still has control. When we entertain his lies, they get a death grip on us.

Here is what the Lord says about your power over the enemy:

> *Listen! I have given you the authority to walk on dangerous snakes and scorpions—even more power than the enemy has. Nothing will ever hurt you!* (Luke 10:19).

> *The "children" are human. So, Jesus also shared in their humanity. He wanted to use death to destroy the Devil who has the power of death. Jesus also wanted to set all people free from the slavery of fearing death all their lives. It is clear that He is helping Abraham's descendants, not angels* (Hebrews 2:14-16).

Everyone has heard about how you obeyed. I'm proud of you. However, I want you to be wise about good, and simple about evil. The God of peace will crush Satan under your feet soon. May the gracious love of Jesus our Lord be with you (Romans 16:19-20).

My little children, you belong to God. You have conquered the false prophets, because the One who is in you is greater than the one who is in the people of the world (1 John 4:4).

*This is why I bow down to the Father. Every family in heaven and on earth gets its name from the Father. I pray that God will use His Spirit to give you power from the riches of His glory to make the person inside you strong. Then, through believing in Christ, He will live in your hearts. You will have your roots and foundation in love. Then you and all of the holy people will be able to completely understand the meaning of Christ's love—how wide it is, how long it is, how high it is, and how deep it is. **It goes beyond knowing**, but you will know it. Then you will be filled with the totality of God* (Ephesians 3:14-19).

THE INDISPUTABLE REALITY: YOUR EXPERIENCE

"It goes beyond knowing." The most powerful weapon you have in your warfare against the world, the mind, and the devil is your testimony. When you know God has done something for you, don't be afraid to say it. Use it as a reminder to yourself in times of future need. It will give you strength and build their faith. Use it with others to help them overcome the lies of the trickster in their walk with the Lord. Use it against the enemy who would want you to forget the good things God has done.

There have been countless times over the years when I was completely at the end of my financial abilities. Each time, I reminded myself that God has always been faithful to see me through.

If your testimony can be stolen away, you have nothing but lifeless doctrine. The proof that the Gospel is true is that it is true in your personal experience. You have lived it. You have experienced it. You know that Jesus loves you, for you have experienced Him for yourself.

Doctrine and theology do not change the world. Our trust and experience is with a living life-force who is greater than anything else in the universe. He has done what we could not do for ourselves. Speaking the word of our testimonies separates us from the systems of religion that want to control what we believe for their own purposes. Before others can experience God's supernatural reality beyond their five senses, believers need to share their testimonies with the world—through their spoken word of God's saving grace, the Holy Spirit can work His redeeming love. When you show others what you have seen, handled, and experienced of this realm of spirit, you give them hope that they can too.

> *But they have defeated him because of the Lamb's blood and because of the message of their testimony. Even when they were about to die, they did not love their lives more than God* (Revelation 12:11).

The blood of Jesus and His testimony overcome satan. It is not doctrine, or a rule for church membership, or our theology. The blood Jesus shed for us on the Cross and the testimony of His followers trump satan each and every time. It is the reality of the Gospel, not the doctrine of the Gospel.

The Old Testament talks about the Ark carrying God's Presence. It was called the Ark of the Covenant or the Ark of the Testimony. The Ark contained the testament or the testimony of the Lord—the Ten Commandments written on stone by the finger of God Himself (see Exod. 31:18). The words were on stone as a type of the stony hearts of humankind that He would redeem for Himself. When humanity yields to the will of God, His commandments are wonderfully and miraculously written on their hearts. We move from natural people to spiritual people, from people with no destiny to people who know why they are born and understand why they breathe.

The Ark of the Presence also contained the testimony of God to the people: Aaron's rod that budded, a jar of manna, and the Ten Commandments. Take away the testimony of the Ark and you remove the God who interacts with His people in a physical *and* spiritual way. God reveals Himself to His people in ways they can understand. *Here is how the prophet Jeremiah describes the reality of the spirit world and God's personal and direct influence upon humanity as individuals:*

> *"Listen," says the Always-Present One, "the time is coming, when I will make a new covenant. It will be with the family of Israel and the family of Judah. It will not be like the covenant which I made with their ancestors. That was when I took them by the hand to lead them out of the land of Egypt. I was a husband to them, but they broke that covenant," says the Always-Present One.*

> *"I will make this new covenant with the family of Israel," says the Always-Present One. "**I will put My teachings in their minds. And, I will write them upon their hearts.** I will be their God, and they will be My people"* (Jeremiah 31:31-33).

EXPERIENCES BEYOND

When we have not yet seen Him in the spirit realm for ourselves, we believe what others say they have seen, what they say they have experienced. Since we have not seen, we sometimes accept the experience of others as the way things really are. We often feel that those with a "spiritual reputation" know better. Our tendency is to accept the words of others even when those words do not feel right within us. Oh, how easily we lay down our own experience at the word of others. How easily we reject what is happening in our own hearts when someone of so-called reputation contradicts what God is doing in us. Remember, discernment is not natural. Even though the discerning of spirits is a gift, it is far different from leading a discerning life. Many things affect the way we discern. That is why we need to be renewed, healed, sancti-fied, and matured. Otherwise, we allow our past, our pain, our politics, doctrines, traditions, fears, and stubbornness to jade our ability to cor-rectly discern. Since I am not sure of another person's spiritual journey, I am extremely careful when being advised by another.

Then again, we do not want to reject another person's words merely because they differ from our experience. God is so big that our experi-ences are bound to be different in many ways. We need to be willing to hear and actively discern the words and experiences of others. Listening to those whom we are sure have our best interests at heart is critical. Of course, 'best interests' have to be defined by all concerned so that you are certain of a counselor's intent.

Personally, I need to be certain of someone's personal love and con-cern for me before I will listen to them. When someone's love for me has been proven in the crucibles of fire and affliction, I can receive counsel with confidence. But these people are few. Respect, author-ity, and confidence cannot be delegated, hired, or assigned; they are earned.

During our earthly journey, God will give each of us unique, per-sonal experiences. We need to stand firm about what He is doing in us and through us, but with the softness and humility of an open and teachable heart. If there is one thing affliction should teach us, it is humility. In affliction we discover not only that we truly are *not* in control but also how badly we need Him to be in control. Our posi-tions are often tested in these trials. They will either cause us to reex-amine what we believe or to stand firm in what we have been taught. Both are essential, for it is fire that burns away what is wood, hay, and stubble in our thinking, and the same fire purifies what is already gold within our hearts.

TESTING WHAT WE HEAR

So it becomes vital to test what is happening inside our hearts to be certain that it is of the Lord. How can you tell the difference between what is of God and what comes from the soul or the flesh? How do you know what to believe? Well, the answer might not be as difficult as it appears. For the discerning, the seeking, and the desperate, the answers are deep in our innermost being where we have touched Him, seen Him, and loved Him. There is a common denominator with a God experience—the Holy Spirit. The Holy Spirit abides within us and teaches us the things that are born of God—and rejects the things that are not. The Holy Spirit renews us and trains our soul in the things of the Spirit. He communicates with us in very tangible, objective ways to lead us into all truth.

THE STEPS OF COMMUNICATION AND DISCERNMENT

First, the Holy Spirit gives us the inner witness of His Spirit. His Spirit bears witness with your spirit. In completely nonreligious terms, the witness of the Holy Spirit is the strong and unavoidable sense of "Yes!" in our spirit. The exhilaration of deep calling to deep, of your spirit touching the eternity of God causes you to be convinced that the thing you have heard or experienced is of God. We must trust the witness within; it is placed there by God. Those who have no idea what it means to have the Holy Spirit leap within often try to discount this awesome heavenly phenomenon. Nonetheless, the Scriptures are clear—His Spirit will witness to your spirit; discernment should be a very normal and trusted part of your daily life. For those who have learned to discern, it is.

Second, hearing a genuine word from God causes a yearning within you to experience the same thing. That testimony becomes salt to us. We become thirsty for what we have heard from another, or what we have heard in our hearts. He draws us deeper into Him with His Holy Spirit placing a yearning for more of Him within us.

Next, these encounters with the Lord stretch and challenge what we have always believed. The Lord is so much more than who we have expected Him to be. Another's experience with the Lord, provided there is a witness of the Holy Spirit, will challenge our doctrines and our traditions. As pointed out earlier, this is a necessary part of genuine growth and maturity. Our softness to the Lord and our brokenness before Him allow us to hear things that we do not want to hear, even though they are truth. Reality always defies the error in our belief systems. The witness of the Holy Spirit gives us the confidence that what we are hearing is true. It gives us courage to change what needs to be changed, thus causing us to grow in our relationship with Jesus.

But we are so human, aren't we? We do not like to be stretched beyond our comfort zones. We thought we had the Lord figured out. We thought of Him within the framework of a manageable theology, but He is bigger than anything we had ever imagined. No doctrine, no theology, and no tradition can keep Him locked in the smallness of our minds. He is a great big God.

UNDERSTANDING THE ENEMY'S TRICKERY

If the enemy of our soul can keep us focused on the five senses, our own pain and troubles, lusts of the flesh, or religion, he will win every time. His only goal is to keep you distracted from your Lord. Your enemy wants you disconnected from your source of spiritual wisdom, spiritual knowledge, and supernatural strength. Because we have been trained since birth to listen to our bodies, we are easily forced out of our spiritual awareness and into all of the enemy's fleshly trickery. Worry, fear, and a host of other fleshy distractions are magnified by the enemy that can throw you into a whirl of mental frenzy that can take months to sort out.

> *The human nature wants things which are against the Spirit. The Spirit wants things which are against our human nature. These oppose each other. Because of this, you cannot do the things that you really intend to do. But, if you let the Spirit lead you, then you are not under the law. Human nature does things which are wrong. These are clear: committing sexual sin, not being pure, having orgies, worshiping false gods, practicing witchcraft, hating people, making trouble, being jealous, becoming too angry, being selfish, making people angry with each other, causing divisions, envying others, getting drunk, having wild parties, and other such things. I warn you now, as I warned you before: The people who do these things will not inherit God's kingdom* (Galatians 5:18-21).

> *We all used to live among people like that, with the evil desires in our human nature. We satisfied the impulses of our bodies and minds. We were like all other people—naturally deserving punishment* (Ephesians 2:3).

It is no wonder we are so tormented when we focus on the things of the natural order alone! Additionally, we must realize that satan is on the same team as the flesh.

It is, therefore, no wonder that the trickster will do all he can to keep you earthy minded. If he can keep you worried, confused, in pain, jealous, envious, lustful, fearful, and so on, you will be stuck in the five senses, far below where you are intended to enjoy life.

But to focus on the realm of Spirit where God is, causes a flow of all that is from the realm of the Holy Spirit, into our body, soul, and spirit. The struggle is clear:

...I serve God's law with my mind, but I serve the sinful law of my body with my human nature (Romans 7:25).

But the solution is equally clear and encouraging:

But the Spirit produces: love, joy, peace, patience, kindness, goodness, faithfulness, gentleness, self-control. There is no law against things such as these (Galatians 5:22-23).

YOU CANNOT GO BACK

The thirst for Him finally becomes overwhelming as we seek Him and see Him for ourselves. It is true you cannot go back. You can no longer play the game of religion. Something has happened that is far greater than the meaningless rituals and monotonous ramblings of a powerless system of religion designed to prevent hungry hearts from truly touching the living God.

If I am to be true to myself and the experience that I have had, I must move on. Let the critics say what they may; I am not here to serve them. I am here to serve my Lord. Let them slander, and accuse, and say all manner of evil against me. I am not here to please them. I am not here to appease them. I breathe for only one reason—to please Him whom my soul loves and to be true to what I have most certainly experienced beyond my five senses. These experiences are by far more real than anything religious programs and presentations can offer. Accolades of men are laughable in the face of Him who called me out of darkness and into His wonderful light.

In this area, the lie of the enemy is most intense, for he plays upon your sincerity of heart and the softness of your love for Him. Heaping false guilt on the believer and blind obedience to authority has been and still is a major tool to keep the hungry from following the Lord. Of course, this is not to say that we do not need authority. But we *do* need authority that is born of the Spirit and is committed to the preparation and launch of the believer and not committed to the continuation and building of a personal kingdom. Only in the heart of the believer can true authority be received. It can never be assigned or imposed. True authority is earned. When it is threatening, demanding, or arrogant, the authority is not from your loving Heavenly Father.

LISTEN AND FOLLOW

I have seen Him. How can I but praise Him? How can I deny the majesty of His glory and the wonder of His mighty acts toward His children? How can I dilute the song He put into my heart and the hope that rings in my spirit? How can I deny the mercy He has shown this worthless sinner or the grace He has poured into my life?

No, I can only talk about what He has done and what I have seen of His love on behalf of mere mortals. I will not be bullied or shamed into denying what has most assuredly happened to this pitiful man. Rather, I will shout it all the more over the housetops of the land. I shall proclaim Him in all His glorious wonder with all the more vigor by whatever means He puts into my hands. Each accusation shall strengthen my spirit, and each contradiction will power my soul.

Will we spend the rest of our lives watching and not becoming? Are we meant to only *see* the age to come? Having seen what we have seen, having experienced what we have experienced, how can anything ever be the same? It is like being carried to the uttermost part of the universe, seeing all there is to see of this dimension; then, being transported from dimension to dimension and seeing what only the angels have seen, returning to earth, and being expected to live as though we have seen nothing. How can that be? How can it happen? Can we really go back to the way it was? No, we cannot.

Something eternal, something other-worldly, and other-dimensional has been planted deep within our hearts, and now nothing is the same. I can't, I won't be satisfied with what is, as though it is what is supposed to be. For *what is*, is merely an aberration of *what should be*, *what can be*, *what God intended*, and, in the dimension of spirit, *what actually is*.

TRICKERY WON'T STOP US

Every word meted out against me shall be strength to my very being and add resolve to my passion. Words intended to bring me pain shall rather bring reassurance that I am doing the will of my Lord. For *what is*, is not *what should be*. The shadow must give way to the form. For the Form is among us. He is here. He moves through us and speaks to us—we cooperate with Him. His Presence is the dynamic that holds all things together, and His love gives life to everything that breathes.

I can no longer be content with this dimension. He has purchased more for me. I will separate myself from the things that try to distract and discourage.

SEEING IS CHANGING

This may be hard for some to believe, but I never saw the ocean until I was 21 years old. Soon after Cathy and I were married, she took me to Long Island, New York, where she grew up. We stood at the ocean's edge, and for the first time I *saw* the glory of the endless sea as it disappeared over *the horizon*. I *felt* the mist on my face and *smelled* its sweet aroma, and my lips *tasted* the salt in the air. I *heard* the sounds of that mighty water lapping onto the shore. My heart was attracted to its depths. I *heard* the beckoning sounds of the waves and the freedom of the gulls as they called to one another along the shoreline teeming with life and majestic in solitude.

I had discovered something that got deep into my soul. I heard the Spirit of the Lord in my heart as He said, *"Deep calls unto deep at the sound of Thy waterfalls"* (see Ps. 42:7). I did not want to leave. I stood there transfixed at the sight of true magnificence and grandeur. I watched as the sun began to set. The last rays changed from yellow, to gold, to amber, to red and finally a striking violet before dipping below the ocean's horizon.

By this time the seaside park had closed, and the beaches were being cleared by dutiful rangers. Cathy was calling to me to come, but I could not move. She did not understand. One ranger began to approach me. I stood still, staring as though hypnotized. He did not understand. Something incredible was happening. Never mind that it happened every day. Never mind that it would be there tomorrow and the next day and the next. I was there. I was witnessing something new, wonderful, glorious. The sun had disappeared over the horizon. The long shadows of the shore disappeared, and the show was over, or was it? The ranger escorted me to the gate, but I could still hear the pounding of the waves and still smell the air and taste the salt. It was there. I just couldn't see it. But I vowed to return to this place again. A vow that I have kept hundreds of times since that first night I saw the ocean. I could no longer be content with life inland. I had to experience my newfound wonder as often as possible. Nothing would keep me from going again and again and again.

This *place* holds a similar eternal wonder. Once you see it, if only for a moment, you are ruined. Nothing else can satisfy. Nothing else fulfills.

Open your heart to this place of Spirit. I had no desire to see the ocean until I saw it. But I was changed forever when I did see it. Some do not understand the attraction to life with God in the Spirit, but it is there. It is calling to us all the time. It is inhabited by all things glorious, all things fulfilling, all things hopeful. Tell the Lord you want all He has for you. Spend time meditating, slowing reading the Book of Psalms (my personal favorite) or any of the books of the Bible that draw you to Him.

Worship is another way that true fellowship is established and ultimately maintained. The most important thing is knowing that God loves you more intensely than you can possibly imagine and wants, more than anything, for you to dwell with Him in the reality of His Presence.

He that has an ear to hear, please listen to what the Holy Spirit is saying, calling out to humanity, wooing His people.

Chapter 3

COOPERATING WITH GOD

He rescued us from the power of darkness and moved us into the kingdom of His dear Son (Colossians 1:13).

GOTTA SERVE SOMEBODY

*G*OTTA SERVE SOMEBODY: *The Gospel Songs of Bob Dylan* is a tribute album released on the Sony/Columbia label in 2003:

You may be an ambassador to England or France,

You may like to gamble, **you** might like to dance,

You may be the heavyweight champion of the world,

You may be a socialite with a long string of pearls

But **you**'re gonna have to **serve** somebody, yes indeed

You're gonna have to **serve** somebody,

Well, it may be the devil or it may be the Lord

But **you**'re gonna have to **serve** somebody.

You might be a rock 'n' roll addict prancing on the stage,

You might have drugs at **you**r command, women in a cage,

You may be a business man or some high degree thief,

They may call **you** Doctor or they may call **you** Chief

But **you**'re gonna have to **serve** somebody, yes indeed

You're gonna have to **serve** somebody,

Well, it may be the devil or it may be the Lord

But **you**'re gonna have to **serve** somebody.

You may be a state trooper, **you** might be a **you**ng Turk,

You may be the head of some big TV network,

you may be rich or poor, **you** may be blind or lame,

You may be living in another country under another name

But **you**'re gonna have to **serve** somebody, yes indeed

You're gonna have to **serve** somebody,

Well, it may be the devil or it may be the Lord

But **you**'re gonna have to **serve** somebody.

You may be a construction worker working on a home,

You may be living in a mansion or **you** might live in a dome,

You might own guns and **you** might even own tanks,

You might be somebody's landlord, **you** might even own banks

But **you**'re gonna have to **serve** somebody, yes indeed

You're gonna have to **serve** somebody,

Well, it may be the devil or it may be the Lord

But **you**'re gonna have to **serve** somebody.

You may be a preacher with **you**r spiritual pride,

You may be a city councilman taking bribes on the side,

You may be workin' in a barbershop, **you** may know how to cut hair,

You may be somebody's mistress, may be somebody's heir

But **you**'re gonna have to **serve** somebody, yes indeed

You're gonna have to **serve** somebody,

Well, it may be the devil or it may be the Lord

But **you**'re gonna have to **serve** somebody.

Might like to wear cotton, might like to wear silk,

Might like to drink whiskey, might like to drink milk,

You might like to eat caviar, **you** might like to eat bread,

You may be sleeping on the floor, sleeping in a king-sized bed

But **you**'re gonna have to **serve** somebody, yes indeed

You're gonna have to **serve** somebody,

Well, it may be the devil or it may be the Lord

But **you**'re gonna have to **serve** somebody.

You may call me Terry, **you** may call me Timmy,

You may call me Bobby, **you** may call me Zimmy,

You may call me R.J., **you** may call me Ray,

You may call me anything but no matter what **you** say

You're gonna have to **serve** somebody, yes indeed

You're gonna have to **serve** somebody.

Well, it may be the devil or it may be the Lord

But **you**'re gonna have to **serve** somebody.

Many years ago, Bob Dylan gave his heart to the Lord. The first song he recorded after that event was one called, "You Gotta Serve Somebody." He had it right. We all serve someone. We serve ourselves, the enemy, the state, or the Lord. We all serve someone. And it is our decision who that will be.

At the end of the day, we will serve somebody.

YOU ARE MORE THAN YOU HAVE BECOME

When you say yes to God, you are agreeing to cooperate with Him. If you say no or maybe, you are actually saying yes to the trickster or your own fleshly and selfish desires.

Every person must decide who to serve, who to love, who to listen to. The fate of the world depends on who we will serve.

"You are more than you have become," Simba's father said to him as Simba ran from his destiny in the Disney movie, *The Lion King*. But the truth is, we are all more than we have become. We all have the capacity, the destiny to soar far higher and further than we could ever imagine. Our spirits yearn for this. Our spirits can see what is there, in the other dimensions of existence. They see what could be if we would but listen with our heart and see with the eyes of the spirit. They know what awaits those who give themselves to the King of all dimensions, the Ruler of all realms.

> *Not only that, but we, who have the first-fruits of the Spirit, groan with pain also. We are waiting to become true sons— when our bodies will be set free!* (Romans 8:23)

To reach our full potential in Him and attain our heart's desire, our goal must be to cooperate with God. Don't allow the lies of the enemy to lure you into complacency. Don't allow him to make you believe you are nothing more than you have already become. It is essential that we trust God and open our hearts to see how He has made us as well as what He has planned for us. Find a place of quiet, far from distraction. Still your heart and your anxious concerns. Wait patiently and expectantly for the Lord, and you will begin to hear Him. Ask Him for insight about how He wants you to cooperate with Him, experience Him, love Him.

How is the enemy lying to you? What are the things holding you back from giving your all to God in this regard? Are you afraid of what He may ask you to do?

Separating yourself from those who think like you, believe like you, and cry out for God like you is a typical ruse of the trickster. We actually feed off one another's spirit and strength. We all know the admonition of Paul when he said, *"and let us think about how we may cause one another to love and to do good things. Do not quit meeting together, as some people are in the habit of doing. Instead, encourage one another even more, since you see the day coming closer"* (Heb. 10:24-25). But make no mistake, Paul did not mean that you should subject yourself to the meaningless rants and rules of religion. Paul was encouraging us to gather with those who have the same passion, love, and desire to serve Him in all His fullness, uninhibited by the rules and traditions of lifeless, religious blather.

So it is essential that you find people who are cooperating with God. Spend time with them. Talk and walk with them. There is safety in the counsel of those who are walking in the same light and sacrificial commitment as you are. These are the people I can trust myself to receive counsel and help from in my search for His will in my life. You will recognize these people by their love and devotion to God's best for you. They will counsel, pray, encourage, and honor you. But they will respect your need to make final decisions and will prayerfully support your decisions in a matter.

CHANGE WILL ALWAYS COME TO THE OPEN HEART

When we decide to trust the Holy Spirit, then He works to direct our focus heavenward. Otherwise, our focus is earthly and of little use to His Kingdom. As we learn to cooperate with God and not to argue with Him, He will change us into who He intends us to be.

Please notice the emphasis here is on the change of the focus of our thoughts. When thoughts are God-ward, we will be in a position to hear and receive from both the natural and the spiritual dimensions. This is how our minds are truly convinced about truth. The Holy Spirit will confirm truth to our hearts. Without the aid of the Holy Spirit, we can only be intellectually convinced of the thing. Therefore, at some point, we can also be "unconvinced." Becoming spiritually attentive is the only way we can be renewed and transformed, not only in our thoughts, but in our way of living as well. When truth is written on our hearts, our change is permanent, indeed.

> *"I will make this covenant with the family of Israel," says the Always-Present One. "I will put My teachings in their minds. And I will write them upon their hearts. I will be their God, and they will be My people. No one will ever teach his neighbor or relatives to know the Always-Present One. This is because **all** people will know Me—from the least important ones to the most important ones," says the Always-Present One. "I will forgive them for the evil things they did. I will forget about their sins forever"* (Jeremiah 31: 33-34).

There are several Scriptures that show us how God wants us to posture ourselves spiritually and thus be able to cooperate with Him.

> *All people who are being led by God's Spirit are sons of God* (Romans 8:14).

> *Trust in the Always-Present One with all your heart. Don't depend on your own understanding. Remember the Always-Present One in everything you do. And He will give you success. Don't depend on your own wisdom. Revere the Always-Present One and refuse to do wrong. Then your body will be healthy. And your bones will be strong* (Proverbs 3:5-8).

And be not conformed to this world: but be ye transformed by the renewing of your mind, that ye may prove what is that good, and acceptable, and perfect, will of God (Romans 12:2 KJV).

*The Spiritual person understands everything, but no one completely understands him: "Who can completely understand the Lord's mind? Who can give Him advice?" But **we** have the mind of Christ* (1 Corinthians 2:16).

IN THE SHADOW OF HIS WINGS

For You have been my help, and in the shadow of Your wings I sing for joy (Psalm 63:7 NASB).

Cooperating with God means snuggling in the shadow of His wings where you will sing for joy. He is your hiding place, your high tower, a fortress in whom you can place your trust. God has proven His love for you. He has demonstrated His power in the lives of those who deserve only the least of His mercies. What other god is like that—who pardons iniquity and passes over the rebellious acts of His children? God does not retain His anger forever because He delights in unchanging love. (See Psalm 103.)

OK. It is time to roll up our spiritual sleeves and get down to the serious business of understanding our enemy and forever putting him in his rightful place—under our feet. Yes, there is a place of spiritual clarity and sober assurance that the enemy of our souls no longer has the advantage in our lives.

The God of peace will crush Satan under your feet soon. May the gracious love of Jesus our Lord be with you (Romans 16:20).

You are from God, little children, and have overcome them; because greater is He who is in you than he who is in the world (1 John 4:4 NASB).

It is certain that in the victory of your Lord and in the reality of the spirit world, the enemy has no advantage over you. However, knowledge is truly power. Knowing who you are, understanding what Jesus actually did on the Cross, and actively taking steps of faith in God are the key prerequisites to a peaceful, fruitful, and joyful life as a believer in Jesus Christ. "The half has not been told" is an incredible understatement when it comes to the depth of love, purpose, and power that is in the heart of the Lord toward you.

Read the following chapters with an open mind and a teachable spirit; nearly every page will be another key to revealing the lies that bind you and unlocking the doors of a wonderful future that cannot be imagined.

THE LOOKING GLASS

All of us have uncovered faces; we reflect the same glory. It comes from the Spirit of the Lord. With one glory after another, we are being changed to look more like Him (2 Corinthians 3:18).

No eye has ever seen this and no ear has ever heard this. No human being has ever imagined this. But this is what God prepared for those who love Him." God used the Spirit to show this secret to you. The Spirit searches everything—even the deep things of God (1 Corinthians 2:9-10).

It sounds too easy to be true. Maybe that is why it seems so hard! We can see the glory of God and the wealth of strength and victory He has for us. Looking into the Spirit will draw us to see by revelation exactly what Paul was trying to tell us through these verses.

Before you can cooperate with God in understanding the lies of the enemy, a new basis of cooperative faith in your heart must begin. The old house of uncertainty and vague doctrine must be demolished. Seeing His fullness is the beginning. Allowing Him to change our thinking is the victory.

There are many things that God really wants to show you, to talk to you about. A good way to begin this process would be to ask a few questions that will show you what God has already done and how He sees you now. These truths will help you change your mind and step into the Spirit of Truth.

1. Where does satan now stand in relation to the Cross of Jesus, and why is that important?

2. Am I the weak, fearful pawn at the mercy of some cosmic battle?

3. Am I really alone in my struggle to follow the Lord?

4. Can God's plan for me really succeed?

Some answers:

1. Satan stands defeated: *"And having spoiled principalities and powers, He made a shew of them openly, triumphing over them in it"* (Col. 2:15 KJV).

2. You are at the mercy of God's grace and forever tied to His love: *"God will always give His mercy to those who worship Him"* (Luke 1:50).

3. You are never alone: *"I will never leave thee, nor forsake thee"* (Heb. 13:5 KJV).

4. You are destined to win, and your victory is now, not just in Heaven: *"But, thank God, through our Lord Jesus Christ, God gives us the victory!"* (1 Cor. 15:57).

Most believers spend most of their time, energy, prayers, and worry trying to stay in God's good favor. It is a tragedy that the truth of God's forgiving power is not clearly taught. This misrepresentation of truth derails so many believers. Even the most devout disciple needs to know and understand that when God says something to him or her from the Word, there is no changing it.

The trickster will keep us lame until we decide to believe, accept, and walk in the truth of God's love.

Let us lay aside these lies and walk on, putting all our strength and power toward God's wonderful plan for our lives.

YOU ARE A SPIRITUAL, MULTIDIMENSIONAL PERSON

After you accept that these answers are true, the lies and deceptions satan uses can be more easily discerned. Remember, you are a spiritual person. Maybe the biggest lie is that you are just flesh and blood without the ability to see or perceive the spirit realm. But nothing could be further from the truth. You are a spirit being. *You are capable of navigating and communicating in multiple dimensions.*

Let us review for a moment. You are a creation composed of three parts. Every person is made up of body, soul, and spirit. Your *body* puts you in touch with the things around you in this dimension of time and space. Your *spirit* puts you in touch with the spirit realm and the dimensions that cannot be touched by the five senses. Your *soul*, your mind, will, and emotions, is the clearinghouse of all the data collected by the five senses and by your spirit. It is in your mind that discernment will either flourish or be dismissed by unregenerate thought processes. It is for this reason that the apostle Paul urges us, *"Don't act like people of this world. Instead, be changed inside by letting your mind be made new again. Then you can determine what is good, pleasing, and perfect—what God wants"* (Rom. 12:2).

How can we possibly understand the things of God, who is spiritual, if we are not spiritually minded? When we give ourselves to the

Holy Spirit, He literally retrains our thinking to accept the data that are collected in the dimensions *beyond* time and space. Up until this point, most of us are taught to dismiss those thoughts, ideas, hunches, dreams, and visions as merely products of the mind. But God will reeducate us, if we allow Him. We will soon discover how consistently God is trying to speak to us. We will be amazed at the volume of data swept into our spirit, much like a fishing net trolling the ocean. The oceans are full of life, and so is the Spirit.

HOLY AND THE PROFANE

A big job of the fisherman is to sort what the net is gathering so he can discard the worthless and retain what is profitable. In the life of believers, the fishing net is our spirit. We gather into the boat, the mind, so the data can be sorted and either used or discarded. Here, then, is why it is so essential to have a strong sense of discernment. As your mind is being trained by the Holy Spirit, you will more readily be able to discern what your spirit has collected.

Too many believers have the erroneous belief that everything that comes to them by way of the spirit realm is born of the Holy Spirit. But the truth is, the spirit realm is full of life, but not all of it useful or helpful. Some of the things we hear are absolute lies and destructive. That is the purpose of this book. The analogy of the fish net is a good one to understand. You may cast your net in an area of ocean that is known for the particular kind of catch you want, but the net will gather not only that but also everything else in its path. Hopefully, there will be more of the fish you want than of the kind you will separate out and throw back into the sea. Our spirits, when yielded to and filled with the Holy Spirit, will collect data for our soul. Discernment instantly determines what is a good catch and what must go. The Holy Spirit is black and white, while religion and our fleshly emotions are very gray. Things always seem to be twilight to the carnally minded.

My son Mathew and his family once stopped at a gas station and snack shop along an interstate highway. His family had just headed for the bathroom when the Holy Spirit told Mat to get out of the gas station immediately. The sense in his spirit was very urgent. He quickly hustled his family back into their truck and drove off. As they drove away, they watched a tractor-trailer run off the interstate out of control. It passed exactly where they were stopped and ran into an embankment. If he had questioned what the Holy Spirit was saying to him, who knows what might have happened.

There is no doubt, we must learn to discern. We must take the time to learn how to sense the Holy Spirit all around us.

EMOTIONS

Sometimes our emotions cause discernment problems. Our emotions are often not under the best kind of personal discipline. Therefore our emotions are drawn toward or repelled from the data gathered by our spirits. Our emotions are mostly just slaves of our past, our pain, and our traditions. Therefore, we are unable to be objective in our discernment. We must not discard our emotions, however. God has emotions. He gave them to us as an important tool of life. God will teach us to control and understand our emotions, and they will become a powerful tool of life. I am not afraid of my emotions, but I work hard to keep them under the Lordship of Christ and the scrutiny of the Holy Spirit, as I try to do with everything else in my life.

Just as children who have been raised to control their emotions properly are more prepared to deal with whatever their spirits collect, we, too, will grow in our ability to harness the strength of our emotions as a wonderful expression of God's life to us.

Believe it or not, religion is another major factor in our inability to discern the realm of spirit. The teachings of Sunday school and the myriad of sermons we have heard drastically affect our emotions as well as our discernment. They mold our thoughts and control what we are allowed to accept. Rather than recognizing that discernment, softness of spirit, and disciplined emotions are necessary to hear the Holy Spirit, many people are content to believe what they are told to believe and what they are told to accept. Believers, therefore, do not know that God is constantly feeding information to them by the Spirit. Nor do they know that they are capable of even receiving such transmissions from the realm of spirit. As a result, if, per chance, the Holy Spirit breaks through this wall of silence to the believer, it is instantly dismissed as an overactive imagination or rebellion of the heart. Much of what could benefit us is instantly refused by our soul due to the lack of teaching and preparation to walk in such multidimensional realities. Thank God that there are those who are hungry enough for the Lord that they are not concerned about the opinions of those who do not share their hunger and have not seen the Lord.

When folks truly forgive, are healed from the wounds of the past, and are freed from the tyranny of religious indoctrination, their emotions can be more readily submitted to the Lordship of Jesus, who will direct their understanding like a master conductor of a heavenly orchestra.

Rather than fearing emotions, or worse, ignoring them, we need to understand that our emotions are an important part of who we are. Only those who are afraid of emotions try to forbid them in the life of the believer. It is amazing to me that folks are free to shout, scream, and make fools of themselves (as our family does in football season), but are forbidden to express such emotions in love and adoration to the Lord. It is ridiculous to think that God gave us emotions we ought to stifle when expressing our love to the Lord.

Hmm, I find it difficult to think that a marriage would last very long if it were not for passion, love, expressive desire, and so on.

LIVE IN THE SPIRIT

Discernment through the Spirit is the only way to recognize the intent of the heart—your heart and others' hearts.

Salvation belongs to the Lord and to His people. We absolutely need to learn the depth and breadth of this mighty salvation. We should strive to experience everything for which Jesus was crucified and raised from the dead. To be satisfied with less than the fullness of His salvation would be to cheapen the value of His love and His sacrificed life on our behalf.

Abundant life is God's plan, and it is the believer's right as a child of the King. The trickster will distract you from this, deny its existence, and destroy your hope in experiencing this fullness of life.

> *Why does the robber come? Only to steal, kill, and destroy. I came, so that they might have life—to the fullest!* (John 10:10)

I have limited confidence in the opinion of the natural mind, which is the fleshly minded part of us that focuses only on the natural realm. This part of our make-up only wants to protect the stubbornness of our own way. Our confidence is in God. This confidence is nothing to be prideful about since it is a hard-learned way of life in our journey to be open and obedient to God. Once you begin to have this confidence, if it is sincere, you are humbled every time you think of your resistance to Him. This confidence is not arrogant because we have all failed so miserably that we need to be forgiven and then *given* the salvation we are incapable of *earning*.

John the Baptist made a statement that has pierced the ages and toppled the kingdoms of devils and men. His proclamation, once and for all, declared the words that God longs to hear from those in whom He dwells. Once John the Baptist had seen the Lord, he proclaimed, *"He must increase, but I must decrease"* (see John 3:30 NASB). So it is with those who truly see Him. The revelation of His mighty love and endless power puts our lives in perspective in relation to His endless mercy toward us. There comes a point in our lives when we see Him for who He really is and who we are apart from Him. Like John the Baptist, we cry out, "He must increase, and we must decrease."

Want to take a big bite out of the enemy's arsenal? See the Lord. Meditate on Him whom your soul loves. You will decrease; He will increase.

SEEK AND YOU WILL FIND

If you cooperate with God, He will clearly show you His will for your life. The moment you say "yes" to Him, God will lead you to your life's most sacred and eternal adventure. It is an adventure that He has dreamed for you from before the beginning of time itself. It will require all your gifts, skills, faith, and determination. But this dream will be the fulfillment of all you have ever desired in this life and the next.

However, you must also understand that if you search for God's will from a selfish perspective, you will not find it. Instead, that self-ishness will allow the enemy to put many good-looking road blocks in your way. We all know what these are. They titillate the flesh, feed our pride, and offer the sense of invincibility and power. The trickster tempted Jesus in this way. Even though Jesus always had pure motives, His motives were put through the fire.

Allow the Holy Spirit to check your heart. This is a most difficult task, for it requires complete honesty. No one sees what happens within the secret place of prayer.

Be honest enough, hungry enough, and principled enough to allow God to tell you things you may not want to hear. If you don't allow God to show you what needs to change, those faults begin to seep through your soul. The discerning will see the real you before anyone else does, and your deception will take hold among those who cannot see the real you. Amidst these dangerous circumstances your fleshly desires will take hold. Many personal kingdoms are built on this sandy ground.

Huts of wood, hay, and stubble are built to resemble grand castles, but the storms of life will blow hard and relentlessly on these feeble, human attempts at greatness. In God's mercy, these manmade castle walls will crumble so the reality of His Kingdom will stand.

> *Be careful! Be sure you listen to the One who is talking to you. God warned the Jewish people, but they didn't listen. They did not escape on earth. If we turn away from God who speaks from heaven, we will be punished even more. At that time, God's voice shook the earth, but now He has promised this: "Once again, I will shake not only the earth, but also heaven!" (The words, "once again," clearly show that things which can be shaken will be taken away. This means things that were made.) Then what cannot be shaken will remain. Therefore, we should be thankful, because we are receiving a kingdom which cannot be shaken. We must worship God in a way that will please Him—with reverence and fear—because our God is like a fire that destroys everything* (Hebrews 12:25-29).

If you allow Him to lead you into the dream He has for you, God's plan for you will most certainly prosper you—bring you honor, recognition, and promotion in His eyes. Truly, He is the only One who matters when it comes to such things as recognition and reward. But God's will ultimately leads to the death of the fleshly, self-serving part of you that wants to be seen, heard, and respected by others. This process causes a remarkable thing to happen in your heart. The honor, promotion, and recognition you receive mean nothing to you as you see yourself as a product of God's mercy. You understand you are a lump of clay that God has transformed into a vessel that is prepared to be used by God. In this alone, will you rejoice. He is increasing. You are decreasing. The power of the enemy in your life is reduced substantially.

Cooperate with God. Follow Him. He will never let you down.

Chapter 4

JESUS, THE GREAT DISCERNER

God's message is alive and active. It is sharper than any sword with two edges. It can slice between the soul and the spirit or between the joints and bone marrow. It can tell the difference between the desires and the intentions of the human mind (Hebrews 4:12).

A Samaritan woman came to get some water. Jesus said to her, "Please, give Me a drink of water." (His followers had gone into town to buy some food.)

The Samaritan woman said to Jesus, "You are a Jewish man and I am a Samaritan woman. Why are You asking me for a drink of water?" (Jewish people don't want to associate with Samaritans.)

*Jesus answered her, "If you knew about God's gift and who I really am, **you** would ask Me to give you a drink of living water!"*

The woman said to Jesus, "Mister, You don't even have a bucket and the well is deep. Where are You going to get this living water? You are not greater than Jacob, our ancestor, are You? Jacob's flocks and herds, his sons, and Jacob himself drank from this well. He gave it to us!"

Jesus answered her, "Any person who drinks this water will become thirsty again, but if anyone drinks the water which I will give him, he will never be thirsty again. The water which I give him will become a spring inside him, welling up to eternal life."

The woman said to Jesus, "Mister, give me some of this water, so that I won't get thirsty and won't have to come back here again and again to get water."

Jesus said to her, "Go, call your husband. Then come back here."

The woman answered Him, "I don't have a husband."

Jesus said to her, "So true! You have had five husbands, and the man you have now is not your husband. You spoke the truth."

The woman said to Him, "Sir, I now understand that You are a prophet. Our ancestors worshiped on this mountain, but you Jews say that Jerusalem is the place where people must worship."

Jesus said to her, "Believe Me, woman, the time is coming when you won't worship the Father on this mountain or in Jerusalem. You Samaritans are worshiping that which you don't understand, but we Jews are worshiping what we know. Salvation comes from the Jewish people. But the time is coming and has now come when the true worshipers will worship the Father in the true, spiritual way. The Father is searching for this kind of people to worship Him. God is spirit. The people who worship God must worship Him in the true way and with the right spirit" (John 4:7-24).

THE REALM OF ALL-GOD

Spiritual discernment does many things. It is the ability to see into the spirit realm, beyond the five senses, discovering God's will, the motivation behind a situation, the spirit that controls a person, his emotions, or his desires. Discernment separates soul from spirit—allowing us to discern the *flesh* and its motivations from the *spirit* of a person and its motivations. But discernment also separates the realm of spirit, which is the entire spirit world, from the realm of living in the Holy Spirit. So we can be in the spirit realm, without being in the Holy Spirit. When I refer to the Spirit realm with a capital "S", I am referring to the realm of the Holy Spirit. A good example of this is the relationship between AOL and the world wide web. If you go on the internet in AOL, you are protected from the evil that is in the world wide web. So, as long you are on AOL when you are on the web, you are safe. This process is learned. Your spirit feeds your soul raw data that is then evaluated, ending in a conclusion that goes far beyond the natural ability to figure out a problem, since the five senses alone do not have the ability to connect with any other dimension. It is a conclusion that is God-breathed and God-empowered. It meets your heart with peace and settles your spirit. This inner peace is the confirmation that you have seen, as well as properly evaluated, the problem.

How can we begin to understand discernment, or receive and interpret the things we hear in the spirit realm? I hope to shed light on this very important topic so that the trickster cannot keep you from accepting everything that is coming to you from God. True discernment will also cause you to see the subtle work of the enemy and give you the wisdom to dismiss his destructive invasion of your life.

TRICKING THE TRICKSTER

You may be surprised to learn that not everything you see and hear in the spirit dimension is of the Lord. As we said earlier, when you drop a net into the water to fish, all kinds of fish can end up in the net. The fisherman must then decide what fish he wants and discard the rest. With a bit of practice, this process is second nature to the fisherman. The same is true in the realm of spirit. Once you begin to develop discernment, you will be able to discard the things that should not be part of the "catch."

Here are some tips:

1. God does not gossip. Strange thought, but very important. God will not tell you things about another simply to give you fodder to spread among friends. If God entrusts you with the deep issues of another, it is an honor, indeed. It is an honor you would do well not to mishandle. The things you see are for the purpose of prayer and nothing more unless absolutely led.

2. The enemy steals, kills, and destroys. When you get data from the spirit realm that does any of these things, reject it outright. The voice of the trickster may sound compassionate, but if the data you get is condemning of anyone, it is not to be trusted. God convicts; we intercede. God speaks in gentle sincerity and love for the sole purpose of redemption. You are not the judge, nor is it your responsibility to deliver a judgmental message; your role is to convey the Father's love. He will do the rest.

3. The enemy will use your weaknesses to deceive you. Be careful of data that feed your weakness or lead you into compromising situations. For instance, the

Lord could lead someone to a bar if they do not have an alcohol problem but would probably not lead a recovering alcoholic into that same situation.

4. The enemy will play on your undisciplined emotions. Maybe you have something against someone. Maybe there is someone you just don't like. The enemy will "give" you a rebuke, correction, or Bible verse apparently for that person. Your dislike for that person will be a juicy temptation to fall into, all in the name of the Lord, of course. That is an old trickster trap that you should never give into.

5. God's words have conclusion. When you can read someone's spirit without giving them hope, encouragement, or conclusion, it is not true spiritual discernment. A diviner can read someone's spirit; only true spiritual discernment can bring godly hope for someone to hold onto.

6. Discernment is first for prayer. You should assume you have been entrusted with something that requires nothing more than your intercessory prayer. This is true spiritual intervention and the highest form of co-labor with God.

7. Discernment can be for prayer, a personal warning, or as a way of being led by the Holy Spirit.

In review, you can be connected to the spirit realm without being in the Spirit. Being in the Spirit is our safety. Sometimes our enthusiasm can cause us to venture into uncharted spiritual territory. By that, I simply mean that we forget that we need to be covered by the Blood of Jesus as well as to be led by the Holy Spirit. The Blood is a shield around us. I am always conscious of the fact that I am in Christ and He is in me. I am protected. I am safe.

Discernment, then, is concluded in the mind, or soul, to use biblical terms. You can receive large amounts of data, but unless you can filter through what you have received and come to the proper conclusion, the data profits you nothing.

"CHECK" IN THE SPIRIT

I am so glad that we serve a God of mercy! I can think of too many times when I did not properly discern the data I received.

We are deeply influenced and often controlled by what we have learned over the years. What we hear from the spirit realm is skewed when it passes through our mind. I have often said that we would be shocked if we could see as clearly in the spirit realm as we can see with our eyes. We would be shocked at what we would find controls the natural realm, that is, the realm of the five senses, where we live.

As someone with a prophetic spirit, I have often seen things that I thought were imminent, only to discover over time that they were not. In the dimension of spirit, there is no time, there is only NOW. God calls Himself the "I AM" (see Exodus 4:14).

Since there is no time in that dimension, everything is "now." Therefore, everything one sees in this realm appears to be imminent. It takes time and experience to know what the Spirit is saying when you see into that realm.

In His infinite mercy and His patience, I am learning how to live in fellowship with my Lord. I am certain that on countless occasions the Lord has had to intervene when I was close to a big mistake. It is not enough that He gives us the ability to both gather and discern information; He even warns us when our discernment is incorrect. The "check" in the spirit, which is best defined as an uncomfortable sense within when we think about something, is the last defense against error. The more we respond to this check, the more sensitive we become to its gentleness and presence. It becomes a source of great comfort and confidence.

Paul and Timothy went through the countries of Phrygia and Galatia. The Holy Spirit did not allow them to preach the Good News in the country of Asia. They went near the land of Mysia. They wanted to go into the country of Bithynia, but the Spirit of Jesus didn't let them go in. So they passed by Mysia and went down to the city of Troas. That night Paul saw a vision. In this vision, a man from the country of Macedonia appeared to Paul. The man stood there begging him, "Come across to Macedonia. Help us!" (Acts 16:6-9).

It is clear that many mistakes I have made could have been averted had I known to discern what I was seeing.

THIS IS NOT MORSE CODE

Some believers communicate the way we communicated a hundred years ago with one another. With Morse code, when you heard the little clicking sounds, you knew someone was talking to you. Eventually, you even found out who it was, but it was cryptic at best. God wants *fellowship, conversation,* and *friendship* with us. He does not want to talk to us with Morse code, smoke signals, or even with a fleece. He wants true friendship. Communicating is hard enough in the best of environments; He does not try to make it more difficult than it has to be. He wants to clearly converse with you. He wants you to understand what He wants and what His plan for you really is.

I will instruct you. I will teach you which way to go. I will guide you and watch over you. So, don't be like a horse or a donkey; they don't understand. They must be led with bits, with bridles, and with reins, or they will not come near you (Psalm 32:8-9).

DISCERNMENT AT HIS COMMAND

Everything in our lives needs to be under the Lordship of Christ. Discernment will often reveal the root cause or the intention of a person's decisions. Discernment must have more power in your life than your personal passions and desires. It must even be greater than the call you have on your life. Your discernment can only have the real value God intends it to if you understand that discernment *is* the Lord Himself directing you. That is why I say it must have the place in your life above your personal pride, goals, and personal kingdom. After all, we are not called to build a monument to ourselves; we are called to build His Kingdom.

Discernment helps to understand why you are getting the counsel you do. Is the intention pure or do they have their own best interest at heart?

In the early days of Destiny Image, there were times I received "prophetic" words from leaders who did not want me to succeed. Some "prophetic" words came from those who wanted me to join their denomination or "fellowship of churches." It was amazing how the check in my spirit stopped me, even though I had no understanding as to why. Looking back, I understand. We pass through and among so many denominations, fellowships, and organizations. To have joined one over another would have limited our effectiveness and our global reach.

Another time I was invited to participate with a group of investors to begin a Christian book distribution company. The investor base was in Europe, but I was to oversee the operation in the United States. After several days of discussion and planning in London, I could no longer dismiss the growing check I had in my spirit. I wanted to do this, but the Holy Spirit was saying no loud and clear. Although I could not understand why, I knew I should obey Holy Spirit's warning. Several months later, I learned that one of the men has absconded with everyone's money. Retirements were lost, life savings were wiped out.

Because I bowed out of the venture, I was spared. Although I tried to warn everyone that it was an ill-fated venture, I was ignored until it was too late.

> *Teach me knowledge and good judgment, because I trust Your commands. Before I received discipline, I used to do wrong. But now I obey Your word* (Psalm 119:66-67).

TRADITION, RELIGION, AND PERSONAL HISTORY

Tradition, religion, and history are three major areas that keep us from true spiritual discernment. If we are not careful, we will be tricked by these most relentless adversaries. The enemy will ruthlessly use these to sidetrack your heart and deter you from your calling.

These three stooges of deception must be marginalized and kept firmly under the Lordship of Christ. That means that tradition, religion, and your past must be under the dominion of the Spirit of the Lord. They must submit to truth. They must obey, giving way to the will of God and the certainty of His purposes. If these big three are not in submission to the Lord, they will rule your life.

> *Be careful! Don't let anyone capture you with philosophy or misleading theories that can fool you. These come from human tradition and worldly standards, not from Christ! The totality of divinity lives embodied in Christ. You are completed in Christ. He is above every ruler and authority. In Christ, you were circumcised with a non-human circumcision. With Christ's circumcision, you stripped away the human nature of your bodies* (Colossians 2:8-11).

Tradition

> *So, the law was our trainer, until Christ came, so that we could be made right with God through faith. The way of faith has come. Therefore, we do not live under the law anymore.*

You were all immersed into Christ. So, you were all clothed with Christ. You are all children of God through faith in Christ Jesus (Galatians 3:24-27).

Many are the traditions of man and culture that stand in the way of the will of God. Our traditions prevent us from moving into the realm of spirit with purity of heart and innocence of spirit. My Italian heritage has many traditions that are directly contrary to the ways of God. Most are rooted in superstition or the occult. There are other traditions rooted in fear and insecurity. Decisions are made and traditions kept purely out of fear.

Of course, not all traditions are bad. A tradition of a holiday family meal, birthday parties, family holidays, and many others remind us of our love and commitment to one another and actually make our relationships stronger and more meaningful. They result in stronger families, communities, and nations.

Religion

There is no power in form. There is no power in mindless ritual. There is no power in repetitious prayer, even Pentecostal repetitious prayer. God does not respond to bells, incense, low lighting, pipe organs, or guitars. He does not dwell in golden boxes on an altar, huge cathedrals, country churches, or wooden shacks. He dwells in sincere and contrite hearts. He moves through people and among those who invite His nearness and covet His friendship.

He does not care whether you meet in a church, a fire hall, or a home. You can sit in pews, folding chairs, or on the floor. You do not need to sit at all. The chairs can be in rows or in a circle. The worship band can be on a platform, on the floor, or the back of the church. He is not attracted or impressed with any of our gimmicks or fleshly attempts to get His attention. He wants you. Present yourself before Him as a living sacrifice, ready to respond to Him with sincerity and faith, and watch the heavens open and feel your heart burn with His manifest Presence.

Be careful of people more interested in the outer appearances. Watch out for those whose lives are double standards, preaching a message of fleshly power but not producing the fruit they demand from you: *"They will hold the outer form of religion, but they say no to its inner power. Stay away from these people"* (2 Tim. 3:5).

Personal History

This is a very subtle but all too common ruse of the trickster. Our past holds incredible sway in our lives. The things we have experienced affect our abilities to love, discern, pray, trust, and believe. Most of us are unaware of the power our past carries in our lives. There is no doubt that the scars of painful times in our past negatively affect our ability to hear from the Lord and move on confidently into the dream He has for us.

Preachers' kids often carry a particularly heavy burden based on how they saw their parents treated and mistreated in the ministry. The anger and hurt they carry as a result of this childhood is often too much to bear in their own search for their Lord. Their personal history is marked by pain, hardship, and abuse from the hands of believers. Unless carefully and lovingly healed, these scars will ruin their ability to serve their Lord and fulfill their own destiny in God.

Our personal history must be under His Lordship so He may gently heal the areas of pain and mistrust that we carry. The trickster is far too adept at using our past as a roadblock to our destiny. We desperately need to submit our hurts to Him daily that He may free us from the things that hold us back. While our past cannot be denied, it can be healed. The truth of His love and the power of His healing touch can free us to reach new heights in our spiritual lives.

The opinions we have, the fears we harbor, the attitudes we carry, and the prejudices we carry are there for a reason. At some point in our lives, we experienced things that caused us to develop into the people we are.

Children of broken homes often have a serious trust issue that prevents them from having a secure marital relationship.

Bad experiences in school cause us to hate certain kinds of people as adults. The list is endless, but to be freed from negative influences is key to properly discerning all we hear in the realm of spirit.

> *He was hated and rejected by people. He had much pain and suffering. People would not even look at Him. He was hated, and we didn't even notice Him. But He certainly took our suffering upon Himself, and He felt our pain for us. We saw His suffering. We thought that God was punishing Him. But He was wounded for the things that* **we** *did wrong. He was crushed for the evil things* **we** *did. The punishment, which made us well, was given to* **Him.** *And, we are healed because of His wounds. We all have wandered away like sheep. Each of us has gone our own way. But the Always-Present One has put upon Him the punishment for all the evils we have done* (Isaiah 53:3-6).

> *Jesus was talking with the Jews who had believed in Him, saying, "If you stay with My teaching, you are truly My followers. You will find out the truth, and the truth will set you free"* (John 8:31-32).

UNHINDERED PRAYER IN JESUS' NAME

Jesus, the Great Discerner, gave us critical instructions about how to keep the trickster out of our prayer life and how to connect directly with God Almighty:

> *Again, I am telling you, if two people on earth agree to ask God for anything, My heavenly Father will make it happen for them. Wherever two or three people have gathered in My name, I am there* (Matthew 18:19-20).

I am telling you the truth: The person who believes in Me will do the same deeds that I am performing. He will do even greater things than these. I am going to the Father. I will do whatever you ask for in My name. The Father will receive glory in the Son. If you ask Me for something in My name, I will do it (John 14:12-14).

If we really can get anything we want by praying in Jesus' name, then there is no reason to learn to hear His voice. Contrary to popular belief, the name of Jesus is not magic.

Prayer is our response to the orders and desires of our King. Prayer is our agreement with His plan. Prayer is not an attempt to convince Him to do what we want done. The whiny, fleshly prayers of a carnal church system do not move God, nor do they plant His Life and Kingdom on the earth.

Remember the words of Jesus, *"I only do what I see my Father in Heaven doing."* And *"If it be possible, let this cup pass from me. Nevertheless, not my will, but your will be done"* (see John 5:19; Matt. 26:39). These are not the prayers of a self-centered church trying to get whatever they want.

Some insist that prayers and Scripture verses need to be repeated again and again. It is thought that we need to claim what we want and storm Heaven's gates. But the King is easy to hear. He is decreeing health, restoration, salvation, and wisdom all the time. If you simply grow quiet in your spirit, you will hear His decree, and then you can shout it from the housetops—not to get His attention, but because He has gotten your attention, and you are finally convinced about what He has said.

When we pray, it is because we have heard the voice of the King. We know that a particular matter will come to pass because we have heard it from the King Himself. We have long ago abandoned the concocted prayers based on our own reason and intellect. Now we only respond to the word of the Lord. Even when it defies reason, we choose to believe Him.

This is genuine Kingdom theology. The fulfillment of our random, sometimes wanton desires was never the intention of the Lord—it is the *modus operandi* of the trickster. When Jesus told His disciples to pray in His name, He knew they would hear His voice and believe, no matter how outrageous what they would hear from Him would be. "Don't be afraid to ask Me," He assured His disciples, "I will do what you are hearing in your spirit. I AM talking to you. You have heard correctly."

> *Thy Kingdom come. Thy will be done in earth, as it is in heaven* (Matthew 6:10 KJV).

When we pray in Jesus' name, we are declaring to Heaven and earth that we have heard from God and He will bring it to pass. Knowing this and praying in His name puts humanity and the spirit world on notice—there is a will and a power greater than theirs. No matter what man or demon is planning, when God speaks, His will comes to pass.

His Word becomes flesh when we hear from Him and pronounce it on earth. This completed circuit releases the power of God and angels to accomplish the decree of the King Himself. When believers pray in His most powerful name, we are declaring that we have heard from the King and are carrying that message to fulfillment. We are certain that God will answer, for we have labored in prayer before the King, and we have heard His voice. We are therefore certain that God will certainly bring it to pass.

PRAYER AND DISCERNMENT

A few years ago, several of us were in intercessory prayer seeking the direction of the Lord in our work. Suddenly the Spirit of the Lord began to speak from deep within. He spoke to one of us that a few needed to go to a certain country for a very specific purpose. Amazingly, two other people were hearing the same precise word from the Lord. Three of us had agreed that we had touched God's heart in the matter. We were confident it was the Lord's will since it was witnessed among us, independently and sovereignly. As we responded in faith, there was a wonderful supernatural result.

In our situation, had there not been a witness among us, we would have needed confirmation to be confident that the Lord was truly speaking.

If our traditional understanding of the verses about praying in Jesus' name is true, why is it that we do not see the results of so many prayers we have prayed in that fashion? Why is it that we do not have the job, the spouse, the car, the house, the clothes, or the ministry that we have asked for in this manner?

We have used these verses in selfish ways. We have believed that if we simply agree on anything we want, He will provide it for us. But in the Most Holy Place, *He* is the center of activity. *He* is the beginning and the end of everything. Our desires have become what He has already desired since the foundation of the world.

Jesus taught us to pray for His Kingdom to come here and now, on this planet, in this and every generation, in our hearts, in good times and in bad. We fully expect the rule and reign of Jesus to be established in the earth, beginning with us. From the beginning of time, it was His plan to redeem for Himself a people for His own possession, a people after His own heart who would be committed to the will of God rather than the will of mere mortals.

"THY KINGDOM COME IN ME"

It is much easier to pray "Thy Kingdom come" when we are praying for the world. The prayer is broad enough that our personal life does not seem to be affected. But when we pray "thy Kingdom come *in me*," we are praying a much different prayer. For now we are asking God to plant His Kingdom seed in us. We are asking Him to use whatever means possible to bring His dream about in our personal lives.

"Thy Kingdom come" is comfortably prayed by folks the world over, but it is prayed without the understanding that God's Kingdom does not come as the kingdoms of men come and go. God is not first looking for territories or land masses. He does not draw geopolitical boundaries when He establishes His rule and reign on the earth.

His Kingdom is first established in much more difficult and hostile terrain—the human heart. His Kingdom is established one person at a time, one confession at a time. Our Lord works out the hardness of our hearts, plants the seed of His love, and then proceeds to remove those things that will most certainly hinder the growth of the seed He has planted.

God's rule is secured in the hearts of people like you and me. His Kingdom is not marked by boundaries as human kingdoms are marked. His Kingdom crosses every border and can be found in every land and language. The King is the only One who teaches us what to do and what to say. He alone gives us permission to speak in His Name, when, of course, we have yielded to Him who rules within and have heard the sound of His voice. He knows what He wants to do and what He wants to accomplish. He knows what He wants to say and who He wants to say it to. He needs neither our advice nor our wisdom. He needs our hearts, our voices, and our willingness to allow Him to do His will through us.

TRUSTING HIM

One of the hardest things for humanity to do is to trust Him. We love to pollute the spiritual atmosphere with our fleshly prayers—you know, the human side of us that whines for our own ways and personal desires. These prayers create smog in the spiritual air and prevent the Lord from doing what is best for us.

"Thy Kingdom come" is a prayer totally devoid of our own selfish desires. It is like a cold wind blowing over the land. It clears away the dust and smoke of our desires and unbelief. It opens the way for the purpose of the Lord to be done in us, through us, and around us.

Our prayers should release the power of Christ to have His way. In my heart of hearts, I can often hear the Lord praying through me. These prayers bring comfort, true exhilaration, and hope. I hear Him calling out to His Father, "Not My will, but Your will be done. I just want what You want." My heart joins Him with prayers like, "Your Kingdom come, not my kingdom. Your will be done, not my will be done." There is no question that the most God-moving prayer we can pray is for His will to be done in our lives and in those around us.

But our tradition of prayer is somewhat different. The first ten minutes is usually spent in a counseling session. We are counseling the Lord about what the problem is and what we want Him to do about it. Then we follow this counseling time with a plea for Him to accept our analysis of the situation. Then we ask Him to do what we have decided is the correct course of action—of course, according to our plan.

We clutter the air with prayers born out of frustration, fear, and uncertainty, as though He needs our wisdom and advice about how to deal with an issue. Then we pray all these things in the name of Jesus. We are certain that if we pray in the name of Jesus, He will do exactly what we want Him to do. After all, we prayed in His name.

But the name of Jesus is not magic. His name cannot be used to invoke the power of God to do the will of man.

Prayer Pause: *Dear Lord Jesus. Thy Kingdom, thy will be done…in me, my family, my church, my community, my nation, and the world. But let your kingdom first come in me. Then may it flow freely to everyone around me. Help me to allow you to have full control in my life. I want you to truly be Lord of my life. Then do with me what you will. Amen.*

IN THE NAME OF KING JESUS

When you pray in the name of Jesus, you are praying in the name of the King. You are praying as a messenger of the will of the King. You are announcing something to the world, both natural and spiritual, that the King wants to happen.

Those who pray in the name of Jesus, the King, are like medieval criers who walked the highways of the kingdoms announcing the will and intentions for the king who rules the kingdom. "In the name of the king, vacate these premises, for the king will build a new castle here!"

The crier cannot cry out unless he has heard the king who sent him. If he has not heard the king, he has nothing to shout out. Many prayers are hollow and empty because they are not prayers at all. They are our own hopes and desires that we are passing off as the decree of the King—except they are spoken without authority or conviction. No one is moved by them, certainly not God.

Everyone believes the crier because he comes in the name of the king. "In the name of the king, all subjects must be on the castle grounds for the coronation of the new queen. In the name of the king, all are expected to attend!"

The one who is pronouncing those words is representing the king. He knows the will of the king and is announcing his will with authority and assurance. He is merely voicing the desire and intentions of the king.

"I come in the name of the king" is the testimony of the medieval crier.

Because we live, for the most part, in the Holy Place instead of the Most Holy Place, that is, in the place of selfish desire and personal greed instead of selfless surrender, our fantasies are in constant conflict with the will of the King, who will always put His plan above our own. He knows that His plan will lead to life, peace, and personal fulfillment beyond our wildest imagination, while our selfish, fleshly plan will only leave us short of His glory.

The Holy Place is a place of personal struggle. It is where we develop our doctrines according to our own hidden desires. These personally contrived beliefs give us assurance that we will be certain to get what we want, at least among men. In the Holy Place, the will of man burgeons out of control, financed by weak and volatile believers who have no strength of discernment or wisdom within themselves. Of course, these Holy Place kingdom-builders count on ignorance to succeed. If true discernment broke out, they would be out of business in a moment of time.

There is only one way the crier can come through town announcing with confidence in the name of the king. He must truly have been in the king's presence. He knows what he is supposed to say because he heard it from the king's lips for himself. Those who have heard the king for themselves will recognize his voice in the words of the crier, and they will be quick to respond to the message he brings to them.

When you hear the voice of the King, you can announce His will with confidence. The Lord awaits those who will hear His voice. He has wonderful dreams to bring to pass—the dreams He has dreamed for you.

This is the secret to having every prayer you utter answered. Listen carefully to hear what Jesus is praying. Then join in His prayer to our heavenly Father, who is waiting for the prayers He will most certainly answer—His own.

Waiting in the wings is the trickster who wants to thwart every prayer you pray or even think about praying. He has become so good at twisting the truth that the world thinks up is down and down is up. You must be aware of his lies so you can resist them.

Chapter 5

SATAN'S LIES

...for Satan is a liar, and the father of lies (John 8:44 NASB).

Be alert! Watch! The Devil is your enemy. He is like a lion. He walks around, roaring and looking for someone to eat. Those of you who are strong in faith must resist him. You know that the brotherhood in other parts of the world is experiencing the same suffering as you are (1 Peter 5:8-9).

PAUL SAID IT BETTER THAN ANYONE ever has. He said, "*...we are not ignorant of* [the enemy's] *schemes*" (2 Cor. 2:11 NASB). The lies we believe have been used over and over again by the trickster. He has nothing new in his bag of tricks. That is why it is important not to be sidetracked by doctrines of demons or manifesting spirits. The only real schemes of the enemy are found in the Scriptures. These alone carry the weight of eternity, and only these deserve study and clarity. Once these lies are recognized and understood, you will be well on your way to discerning his tricks and resisting them in the power of the Holy Spirit.

The following passage of Scripture graphically illustrates many of satan's lies—lies he used on Jesus and continues to use on all believers throughout the ages.

> *Then the Spirit led Jesus into the desert to be tempted by the Devil. Jesus did not eat anything for forty days and nights. After this, Jesus was very hungry. The Devil came and said to Jesus, "Since you are the Son of God, command these rocks to become food."*

> *Jesus answered, "It is written: 'A person does not live on food alone. Instead, he lives on every word which comes from the mouth of God.'"*

> *Then the Devil took Jesus into the holy city, Jerusalem, and put Him on a very high place of the temple. He said to Jesus, "Since You are the Son of God, jump off! Because it is written: 'God will command His angels to take care of You.' And, 'Their hands will catch you, so that you will not hit your foot against a rock.'"*

> *Jesus answered him, "But this is also written: 'You must not test the Lord your God.'"*

> *Suddenly, the Devil took Jesus to a very tall mountain and showed Him all the kingdoms of the world and the glory which was in them. The Devil said to Jesus, "I will give you all of these things, if You will only bow down to worship me."*

> *Then Jesus said to the Devil, "Go away, Satan, because it is written: 'You must worship the Lord your God. Serve only Him.'"*

> *Then the Devil left Jesus. Immediately, angels came and helped Him* (Matthew 4:1-11).

LIE #1 "YOU ARE COMPLETELY ALONE!"

Isolation

Then the Spirit led Jesus into the desert to be tempted by the Devil (Matthew 4:1).

Satan tells you that you are isolated with your problems. There is no one who can help you.

But there are countless other believers struggling with the same things that you struggle with. Sometimes we try so hard to be spiritual that we never tell even our closest friend that we are in trouble. You are not alone. We all struggle. We all need His grace. There is no one exempt from the temptation of sin, whether it be depression, lust, greed, envy, or a myriad of other possibilities. Those who are honest with themselves and with the Lord are quick to admit the temptation, confess the sin, and receive the forgiveness of the Lord. This is the only way to be rid of the weight of sin, guilt, and remorse. Blaming someone else for your sin will only add to the weight of guilt. At the end of the day, I alone am responsible. Putting the blame where it belongs, on yourself, and repenting will once and for all set you free. It is at this point that your isolation fades away, for the sense of His Presence and well-being returns to your heart.

Thy kingdom come. Thy will be done in earth, as it is in heaven (Matthew 6:10 KJV).

Whom resist steadfast in the faith, knowing that the same afflictions are accomplished in your brethren that are in the world (1 Peter 5:9 KJV).

Remember, I will always be with you even until the end of time! (Matthew 28:20)

God Himself has said this: "I will never leave you. I will never abandon you" (Hebrews 13:5).

For some reason, it is difficult for us to believe that He can love us in spite of our failures. But thank God He is not like us. He does not have a fallen nature that reacts to us as we so often react to one another. He is perfect—so is His love for us. It seems ludicrous to say, but He is far more trustworthy than the enemy of our soul, yet we tend to believe the enemy before we believe our Lord. God help us to accept His love, forgiveness, and mercy as quickly as He gives it to us!

LIE #2 "YOU ARE WEAK AND HELPLESS!"

Satan tells you that you are tired and weak—that you are not able to resist him.

> *Jesus did not eat anything for forty days and nights. After this, Jesus was very hungry* (Matthew 4:2).

Truth is, we sometimes do become very tired. It is also true that we have a harder time resisting the trickster when we are tired and weak. We can minimize his ability to attack us when we are in this condition by being careful to get the rest we need. There is nothing spiritual about working ourselves to exhaustion. In fact, the possibility of doing fleshly religious work producing wood, hay, stubble, and all things burnable is greatly enhanced if we do not take the time to wait for the Lord, being renewed in His Presence and filled with His Spirit and strength. We can hear Him more clearly in rest and peace, not in the flurry of fleshly endeavor. None of us want to waste time building something that will have to be dismantled in order to build His Kingdom. Maintaining a good rest schedule is critical if we want to do only what the Lord leads us to do.

> *But the people who trust in the Always-Present One will become strong again. They will be able to soar as an eagle in the sky. They will run without needing rest. They will walk without becoming tired* (Isaiah 40:31).

It is vain for you to rise up early, to sit up late, to eat the bread of sorrows: for so He giveth His beloved sleep (Psalm 127:2 KJV).

LIE #3 SATAN TELLS YOU THAT ONLY HE CAN SATISFY YOUR HUNGER

The Devil came and said to Jesus, "Since You are the Son of God, command these rocks to become food" (Matthew 4:3).

In a way, the trickster is correct. He is the only one who can satisfy your hunger…for sin and its wanton gratification. The writer of Hebrews advised the Church to endure troubles rather than indulge the *"pleasures of sin for a season"* (Heb. 11:25 KJV). The enemy cannot satisfy the true desires of your heart, only the temporary, fleeting pleasures of sin that end in disappointment, shame, and loss.

The next time the enemy tries to tell you that only he can satisfy your desires, read these verses and turn your heart toward the Lord, who instantly gives you strength.

Jesus answered, "It is written: 'A person does not live on food alone. Instead, he lives on every word which comes from the mouth of God'" (Matthew 4:4).

But these, as natural brute beasts, made to be taken and destroyed, speak evil of the things that they understand not; and shall utterly perish in their own corruption; and shall receive the reward of unrighteousness, as they that count it pleasure to riot in the day time. Spots they are and blemishes, sporting themselves with their own deceivings while they feast with you; having eyes full of adultery, and that cannot cease from sin; beguiling unstable souls: an heart they have exercised with covetous practices; cursed children: which have forsaken the right way, and are gone astray, following the way of Balaam the son of Bosor, who loved the wages of unrighteousness (2 Peter 2:12-15 KJV).

LIE #4 "GOD MUST PROVE HIS LOVE!"

Satan tells you that God must prove His love to you.

He said to Jesus, "Since You are the Son of God, jump off! Because it is written: 'God will command His angels to take care of you.' And, 'Their hands will catch you, so that you will not hit your foot against a rock'" (Matthew 4:6).

But the greatest proof of God's love is what He already did on the Cross. Our faith is not based on the volume of miracles He does or recognizable answers to prayers. Our confidence and assurance is steady simply because He is faithful. In fact, He is so faithful; He is for us even when we fail Him: *"If we are not faithful, He is always faithful, because He must remain true to Himself"* (2 Tim. 2:13).

Jesus answered him, "But this is also written: 'You must not test the Lord your God'" (Matthew 4:7).

The enemy knows that if he can get you to doubt God's faithfulness, you will be like a ship without an anchor in a stormy sea. Paul spent much of his time trying to overcome this lie that affects as many people today as it has through the ages:

But God commendeth His love toward us, in that, while we were yet sinners, Christ died for us. Much more then, being now justified by His blood, we shall be saved from wrath through Him. For if, when we were enemies, we were reconciled to God by the death of His Son, much more, being reconciled, we shall be saved by His life (Romans 5:8-10 KJV).

It is good to remember that the best defense against the lies of the enemy is to know the Word. The truth is what God says about you as well as what He says about Himself. The words of the enemy are lies.

LIE #5 THE TRICKSTER HAS WHAT YOU WANT

Lie of Possession

Suddenly, the Devil took Jesus to a very tall mountain and showed Him all the kingdoms of the world and the glory which was in them. The Devil said to Jesus, "I will give you all of these things, if you will only bow down to worship me" (Matthew 4:8-9).

The enemy cannot give you something that he does not own. The truth is, he has nothing you need. He has nothing that can bring you to true purpose and fulfillment. Everything he gives comes with the price of separation from God. Everything he offers is temporary, fleeting at best. He is betting on your desire for temporary satisfaction at the expense of experiencing the Presence of the Lord in the here and now. Everything the enemy has to offer is destined to perish. It is burnable and temporary. It has no possibility of anything eternal, except pain and suffering that leads to death, not life.

Satan tells us that he owns the world, that if we want anything, we need to serve him. He is such a liar. I don't understand how we all fall for this stuff so much. Hey, you are not alone. Just because I am writing a book does not mean I do not have struggles and temptations. I am just like anyone else. We are fellow strugglers in our desire to love and serve our Lord in the fullness of His Life and power and love.

So let's check out what the Bible says about this. In reality, the enemy owns nothing. He is a pauper, a thief, and genuine trickster with no hope of redemption and no power or ownership over *anything*. We are Kingdom heirs because of Jesus' sacrifice on the Cross.

We already have everything. Bargaining with the enemy reveals that we really do not believe what God has for us. That is why when someone sells out to the devil, it is such a divine insult. We already *"own the cattle..."* (Ps. 50:10). We already are kings and priests, already have the power of demons, weather, and everything created. The multidimensional work of the Cross has made us kings in every way.

> *But ye are a chosen generation, a royal priesthood, an holy nation, a peculiar people; that ye should show forth the praises of Him who hath called you out of darkness into His marvelous light: Which in time past were not a people, but are now the people of God: which had not obtained mercy, but now have obtained mercy* (1 Peter 2:9-10 KJV).

> *And they were all amazed, and spake among themselves, saying, What a word is this! for with authority and power He commandeth the unclean spirits, and they come out* (Luke 4:36 KJV).

> *Verily, verily, I say unto you, He that believeth on Me, the works that I do shall he do also; and greater works than these shall he do; because I go unto My Father* (John 14:12 KJV).

You Will Serve Someone

In Luke 4:7, the devil said to Jesus, "It will all belong to You, if You will only bow down in front of me." You will serve someone. Serving the trickster or yourself will lead to disappointment and ultimate failure. Serving the Lord will lead to eternal life in His most excellent Kingdom.

> *because it is written: "God will command His angels to take care of you"* (Luke 4:10).

"It will all belong to You, if You will only bow down in front of me." Jesus answered him, "It is written: 'You must worship the Lord God. Serve only Him'" (Luke 4:7-8).

Jesus answered him, "But it also says: 'You must not test the Lord your God'" (Luke 4:12).

Warning From the Word of God

The Devil finished tempting Jesus and went away from Him to wait until a better time (Luke 4:13).

Jesus told the disciples not to rejoice because they had power over the enemy, but because their names were in the Lamb's Book of Life. Jesus knew that the enemy always comes back. "Don't get cocky," He really said to them. "Stay on the alert, for your adversary is on the prowl."

The Scriptures warn us at the end of this event that although Jesus successfully resisted satan, he would certainly come back at a more opportune time. The problem for the trickster was there was no more opportune time. The enemy tempted Jesus at His most vulnerable state—hungry and tired—and still He defeated the adversary.

Be alert! Watch! The Devil is your enemy. He is like a lion. He walks around, roaring and looking for someone to eat. Those of you who are strong in faith must resist him. You know that the brotherhood in other parts of the world is experiencing the same suffering as you are. God called you into His eternal glory in Christ. After you have suffered a little while, the God of all gracious love will make you complete, strong, firm, and solid (1 Peter 5:8-10).

LIE #6 YOU CAN HAVE VICTORY WITHOUT SUFFERING

From then on, Jesus began to show His followers that He must go away to Jerusalem; that the Jewish elders, the most important priests, and the teachers of the law would make Him suffer many things; that He would be killed, but on the third day, He would rise from death. But Peter came to Him and began to correct Him, "This will never happen to You, Lord!" (Matthew 16:21-22)

This is such an interesting passage. Here we see the up-close confrontation between our Lord and His enemy. The devil used Jesus' close confidant, Peter, to tempt Him with kingship without the suffering that the Father showed Him He would have to experience. Hmm…we all know that Jesus never sinned, but here we see that temptation got close to Him. Here was the issue with which He was most concerned—His crucifixion. The enemy got so close to Him! Talked to Him through His best friend! Jesus, of course, saw right through it. But He had to act. He had to distance Himself from the temptation. So He had to speak out. The enemy used Peter's pity, love, and ignorance of the need of the crucifixion to speak to the Lord. As soon as Jesus rebuked him, it cut off the connection Peter had with satan and abruptly ended the temptation.

The enemy will attack your most vulnerable places. He will exploit the weaknesses in your life to try to get to you. If that doesn't work, he will send a well-meaning friend to help him out. Real friends will never be the tool of the enemy in your life, but they are often unwitting accomplices in the enemy's plan to sidetrack you from God's plan.

The liar tells us that we can have victory without pain, resurrection without crucifixion. He tries to convince us that the Lord makes life too hard, that following Jesus is too much to ask.

Folks who tend to believe this line of reasoning have not matured enough to understand that life is difficult. In fact, life without the Lord is most difficult indeed. Over the years, Cathy and I have wondered how folks survive without having the Lord as their strong defense, their protection, their hope. We can tell you from the personal experience of raising five sons that trying to keep track of their comings and goings without the knowledge that the Lord is guiding us and protecting them, would have been far harder than it was. Even with the Lord's nearness and the guidance of the Holy Spirit, it was difficult.

So what is the point? Life will be difficult whether or not you follow Jesus. But with Jesus, you have His Presence, His counsel, His mercy and lovingkindness, and the confidence that you are doing what you need to do. Of course, He does not abandon those who do not trust Him. His Holy Spirit is striving with all men to bring them into the saving knowledge of His grace.

"Yet man is born unto trouble, as the sparks fly upward" (Job 5:7 KJV). Troubles cannot be avoided. That is the bare truth. Anyone or anything that tells you otherwise is deluded, for sure.

The Word of God tells us that there will be suffering for His sake. Jesus Himself was not immune to the need for suffering: *"Even though Jesus was God's Son, Jesus learned to obey from the things He suffered"* (Heb. 5:8).

The lies we believe are all rooted in the avoidance of pain, suffering, and grief. They exempt us from personal responsibility to the Lord and those we love. Here are more lies we need to be aware of and learn to deal with. Remember, I am using so many Scriptures because, ultimately, His words, not mine, will set you free.

LIE #7 SATAN TELLS US THAT WE DON'T HAVE TO BE HELD ACCOUNTABLE

Then Jesus said to His followers, "If anyone wants to follow Me, he must carry his cross and follow Me. He must say no to himself. The person who wants to save his life will lose it, but every person who gives his life for Me will find it" (Matthew 16:24-25).

I often wondered why Jesus followed His rebuke of Peter with these two statements. Jesus knew that Peter was not happy that he was rebuked by his Lord. But Jesus knew that Peter would have to take responsibility for his words and for his attitudes. Even our love needs to be under the Lordship of Jesus. What? How does love work under the Lordship of Jesus? Why does love need to be controlled? It doesn't. Our emotional response to love needs to be under control of the Holy Spirit. The secular world calls it "tough love." Love's response to a particular situation is sometimes emotionally the opposite of what we normally equate with love.

The enemy will confuse emotional love with God's love every time. He will send us those who will sympathize with our circumstance just when we should not have pity or sympathy. When someone comes along and comforts us when we need to repent, we find that we have unnecessarily prolonged a difficult time in our lives. When we need to repent of something, repentance is the fastest way to get back into the right frame of heart and mind. Repentance alone will bring the resolution we know we need.

> *Happy is the person whose sins are forgiven, whose wrongs are pardoned. Happy is the person whom the Always-Present One does not consider to be guilty. In that person there is nothing false. When I kept things to myself, I felt weakness deep inside me. I moaned all day long. Day and night, You tested me. My strength was gone, as in the summer heat. Then I admitted my sins to You. I did not hide my guilt. I thought: "I will confess my wrongs to the Always-Present One!" And, You did forgive my sins. (Selah) For this reason, let each one who is godly pray to You while they still can. When troubles rise up like a flood of huge waters, they will not reach that person. You are my Hiding Place. You protect*

me from my troubles. You surround me with songs of victory. (Selah) (Psalm 32:1-7).

LIE # 8 YOU CAN GET WHAT YOU WANT WITHOUT SUFFERING

It is certainly the trend of modern society and human nature to want something, anything, for nothing. From the lottery to free products to government programs, folks naturally gravitate to free stuff. But in the Kingdom of God, there is no shortcut. The glory prepared for us is not free. It came with a price, a huge price, the life of the Son of God. So it is with us. The Life of Christ within grows as we die to the desires and temptations of the natural man. Every time we resist the temptations presented to us, we die a bit more, and God's life grows stronger within. This is the price we pay for all God's dreams for us. We die daily so we may have the eternal life of God right here and now. Every time you refuse the tempter, you are exercising your faith in the new life of Christ within. Every act of resistance to the enemy and submission to the Lordship of Jesus is an act of pure, raw worship to the Father. He sees it, loves it, rewards it.

> *That's why we never give up. Even though our physical bodies are wearing out, our spirits are getting younger every day. The troubles we now have will last only a short time. They are working out a far greater eternal glory for us, which is worth so much more than what we are suffering now. We shouldn't look at things which can be seen. Instead, we should look for things which cannot be seen. What is seen is only temporary, but what is unseen lasts forever* (2 Corinthians 4:16-18).

> *And Jesus answered them, "Have faith in God"* (Mark 11:22).

LIE #9 GOD WILL NOT HEAL YOU

Satan tells us that God will not heal you.

> *Jesus was teaching in one of the synagogues on the Sabbath day. In that synagogue there was a woman who had a spirit that made her sick for 18 years. Her back was always bent; she couldn't stand up straight. When Jesus saw her, He called to her, "Woman, your sickness has left you!" Jesus put His hands on her. Immediately she was able to stand upright. She began to praise God. The synagogue leader was angry, because Jesus had healed on the Sabbath day. The leader began to say to the crowds, "There are six days for work. So, come to be healed on one of those days. Do **not** come for healing on the Sabbath day!" The Lord Jesus answered, "You hypocrites! All of you untie your ox or your donkey from the stall and lead them to drink water every day—even on the Sabbath day! This woman whom I healed is our Jewish sister, but Satan has held her for 18 years. Why can't **she** be untied from her sickness on the Sabbath day?" When Jesus said this, all the people who were opposing Him felt ashamed of themselves. The whole crowd was happy. They were thanking God for the wonderful things Jesus was doing* (Luke 13:10-16).

Religious Restraint?

I don't think I will ever understand how some can teach that Jesus will not heal, or that the healing was done in a manner that was somehow incorrect. Some act as though God is impersonal, that the Bible acts independently of the Lord. They seem to have no concept that if a healing occurs in Jesus' name and at His leading, then Jesus did the healing. It is the only way it works. If we cannot trust the name of Jesus, we are a people most to be pitied. If we have to worry that our prayers are being answered by anyone else but Him when we pray in His Name, we are finished. God is bigger than our theology. He is bigger than the capacity of our minds to comprehend the awesome splendor and love of God.

When religion tries to control the flow of the Spirit and power of the Lord, then we can be certain that it is a lie from the enemy. The devil will try to convince the most devout as well as the truly sincere that He does not do the things that have historically and eternally demonstrated among us that He is the Lord. Whenever someone tells you that God doesn't, can't, won't, it is time to look carefully.

> *You know about Jesus from Nazareth. God anointed Him with the Holy Spirit and power. Jesus went everywhere doing good things for people. He healed everyone who was ruled by the Devil. God was with Jesus* (Acts 10:38).

> *But He was wounded for the things that we did wrong. He was crushed for the evil things we did. The punishment, which made us well, was given to Him. And, we are healed because of His wounds* (Isaiah 53:5).

> *This woman whom I healed is our Jewish sister, but Satan has held her for 18 years. Why can't **she** be untied from her sickness on the Sabbath day?* (Luke 13:16)

> *Jesus Christ is the same yesterday, today, and forever* (Hebrews 13:8).

LIE #10 WE WILL SELL OUR INTEGRITY FOR A PRICE

> *One of Jesus' twelve apostles was named Judas Iscariot. Satan entered Judas. He went off and talked with the most important priests and some of the soldiers who guarded the temple. Judas talked to them about a plan he had to hand Jesus over to them. They were pleased. They agreed to give Judas some money* (Luke 22:3-5).

Peter asked him, "Ananias, why did you let Satan fill your heart? You lied to the Holy Spirit. You misused the sale price of the land" (Acts 5:3).

There is one place where folks can be hit hard—their wallets! The enemy knows this weakness well and uses it wherever he can. We must be certain that we hold the truth of the Lord deeply enough that we cannot be persuaded by money to give ourselves to the work of the enemy and the flesh. The warnings against the love of money are astounding. The Lord urges us to satisfy our hearts with Him and all He gives us in friends and family. When our satisfaction is in Him, we will not be deluded by this awful lie.

Learn the truth and never reject it. Get wisdom, self-control, and understanding (Proverbs 23:23).

…Who can live near this fire that burns on and on? A person might do what is right. He might speak what is right. He might refuse to take money unfairly. He might refuse to take money to hurt others. He might not listen to plans of murder. He might refuse to think about evil (Isaiah 33:14-15).

For the love of money is the root of all evil: which while some coveted after, they have erred from the faith, and pierced themselves through with many sorrows. But thou, O man of God, flee these things; and follow after righteousness, godliness, faith, love, patience, meekness (1 Timothy 6:10-11 KJV).

Chapter 6

HIS WAYS—NOT OURS

No eye has ever seen this and no ear has ever heard this. No human being has ever imagined this. But this is what God prepared for those who love Him (1 Corinthians 2:9-10).

G OD SEES THINGS DIFFERENTLY from the way we see things. Sometimes what we see gets real scary, even frightening. This isn't bad. We are afraid of these new things because they are things we have never seen before, or thought of before. New frontiers are frightening, but also exhilarating. They challenge our comfort zones and show us new horizons.

But new things are essential if we are to move on in Him. A favorite lie of the trickster says there is nothing new under the sun, so don't try anything different from what you have been taught. While it is true that there is nothing new in God; for us mortals, everything is new. Every day there are new adventures, new revelations, new understandings of His vast universe. We need to see the Bible, not as a pantry with everything in its place, but as a window through which we see eternity. Every time you open the Bible, there are new discoveries, new wonders to explore. Too many people see the Bible as our spiritual encyclopedia, where everything is explained and laid out to see and believe. But in truth, we should see the Bible as our spiritual Hubble telescope, always exploring the boundless horizons of our eternal God.

Jesus broke the mold of the doctrines of the Jewish religion. He turned their world upside down by the things He taught and demonstrated. He made them look outside their belief system, their theology, their doctrine, and their particular sect of Judaism.

How many times do you think the ancient Jews saw somebody healed by having mud made from spit rubbed in his eyes? Before Jesus did it, how many times do you think they saw that happen? What would happen if I grabbed some dirt, spat in it, walked around, and slammed it on people who have deaf ears, blind eyes, or a stuffy nose?

And yet when Jesus did the unthinkable, He brought sight to a blind man. We think we're so much more sophisticated now than they were back then, so it wasn't such a big deal to "hock a loogie," rub dust in it, and smear it in someone's eyes. But this wasn't an everyday occurrence, and it was at least as marginally disgusting then as it would be now—except for the fact that Jesus did it.

And how about John the Baptist making a passionate plea for people to repent and be baptized? In the midst of his passionate plea, the Pharisees come to be baptized. Here is John the Baptist with his wild eyes, his hair all over the place, and his beard matted with honey, dust, and locust pieces. He's preaching at the riverside when he sees the Pharisees coming forward to repent and to be baptized. John the Baptist, instead of being overwhelmed with joy at this amazing turn of events, looks at them and shouts, "Who warned you to flee from the wrath to come?"

They looked at him, undoubtedly a bit startled, and said, "You."

"Well then you better bring forth the fruit that proves you are repenting," was John's ungrateful response (see Matt. 3:7-9).

Now if a bishop or somebody very important were to answer an altar call today, how many people would be happy about that? We'd have them on television tomorrow morning! But God does things in unexpected ways. When we expect Him to do things our way, and it doesn't happen, we resist Him.

Before the spiritual awakenings in Pensacola, Florida, and before Toronto, there were millions of Christians who were fasting and in prayer, seeking God for revival and a great harvest. But as soon as God started to answer those prayers, guess what? Many people who prayed earnestly for revival and renewal resisted it. This was true with the outpouring in Lakeland, Florida. When renewal does not happen through us, or in the way we think it should using the men and methods we think are right, it is called fleshly and demonic. God help us to see outside our boxes of tradition, pride, and doctrine. Oh God, do whatever You want in whatever way You want, using whomever You want, whenever You want!! Give us eyes to see through all the stuff of the flesh and lies of the enemy so we can rejoice and participate in your work in the earth today. Amen!!

HIS STRANGE WAYS

When God comes in the door, sometimes He comes in strange ways. Sometimes He uses the strangest-looking and strangest-sounding people because He is not interested in our attachment to the outward appearance; He's looking for a people who can hear, understand, and recognize Christ from within. He's seeking people who can look beyond the outward appearance and see Jesus.

A few years ago, there was a big ruckus in our city because the Hare Krishna people were going door to door evangelizing—my sons used to call them "hairy Christians" because they couldn't pronounce Hare Krishna. But when they came to our door, one would jump up and down pounding a little tambourine, while the other one wanted to hand us a flower and a tract explaining their faith.

It didn't take a lot of discernment to realize that they weren't Christians. But what happens when two guys in two-piece suits come knocking on your door, hand you a Bible, and tell you that Jesus loves you? Then you need discernment; you need to be able to see into their heart of hearts. You need to be able to discern what they are telling you, what they believe about the Bible and Jesus.

Many believers have lived a life of external Christianity, satisfied with the facade of religion and missing the power of God. He wants to change us from within and make our lives truly worth living. He is not interested in how big our churches are. He is interested in people who are prepared to carry Jesus, who is living inside of us, to the four corners of the earth.

I AM POSSESSED; YOU SHOULD BE, TOO!

I am possessed. You think I'm strange. Think out of your box. I am possessed. Some of you have probably realized by now that you're possessed too. But you have learned how to control this entity from another dimension (Christ). You have been taught, trained, and conditioned to believe that this Christ has come to serve your every need, to give you what you want, to wait quietly within you like an obedient genie in a magic bottle. When you need something, you simply call on Him, and He runs to the rescue.

You are right: He is within and cares for all our needs. But this is not why we are called to be His disciples.

We forget that we let Him possess us in the beginning, so that *we* could serve *Him*. Instead, we have made Him our servant. There is a powerful and exciting way of life waiting for all who understand that this Jesus within just wants *out* to live the life He wants to live through you.

Our job in the Church is to help explain how to let Christ within us out into a hurting world. How do you yield to the Christ of God within? How do you let Him have control? How do you learn to hear His voice instead of your own voice? How do you learn to let Him direct you, instead of going your own direction in your own way?

Becoming centered on Jesus Christ is the beginning of the adventure. Listening to Him instead of the trickster causes us to be totally involved with the work of Jesus instead of the work of the flesh.

GIVE HIM A HUG FOR ME

Unfortunately, we have turned this holy Alien Force who was sent to us to accomplish His universal plan on this planet into something He never intended. We have twisted and turned the entire plan to make *us* the center of our universe rather than keeping the Force as the most important source of light and life. To most believers, the world is still flat, and the entire universe revolves around us—we are the most important things that ever breathed air.

Meanwhile, we have no joy; we have no peace; there is emptiness inside, and we wonder, *how can this Christ of God be inside of me if I'm still so miserable?* If I'm not talking about you, forgive me; I'll make my own confessions.

Why am I so lonely? Why am I so confused if this Christ of God was supposed to do so much for me? And yet, what we need to discover is that He is not here for our pleasure. We are here for His pleasure. The greatest joy in life is not having this entity jump when we need something; it is hearing the Christ of God say, "Nori, I want you to do something." How will I respond to that? Am I going to resist that call from my Lord? I don't think so. You've got to be kidding—God just said He wants me to do something!

And my greatest joy is doing what He's telling me to do. My greatest pleasure is giving Him pleasure; I respond, "Here I am, Lord, use me. Here I am, Lord, have Your way. Here I am, Lord, do Your thing inside of me."

"Nori, that old guy needs a hug; hug him for Me." And when you hug him, you know what? You can feel God's presence slip in.

We're going to get out of our religious jumpsuits here, and let Jesus be Jesus, and let us be the children of God we are meant to be. I believe the Bible is the inspired Word of God, amen. He never violates His Word; He never does anything against His Word, *but* He violates what this puny brain thinks about God's Word seven days a week.

Many have spent a lifetime having doctrine drilled into their brains so that they can't tell the difference between the Word of God and what they have been told.

The early theologians of the second and third centuries made a point of recording meetings when the saints gathered together. Once a year, theologians got together from hundreds of miles away to study the journals of previous meetings to determine if what they believed was accurate according to what God was doing in the meetings.

They believed in the *reality of the living God* so much that if they had a doctrine that violated what happened in the meetings, they changed their doctrine. Isn't that incredible? The original church leaders had only one desire. They wanted the truth of the living God to be experienced among them. Their own egos were not important. They simply changed to allow God to do what He wanted among them. It is a far cry from today. For now there is a greater interest in preserving doctrine, even to the point of denying the move of God when it violates what we believe.

PEA BRAINS

I had to go to London for a publishing meeting; at the last minute I canceled, and one of my assistants went. I had given a physical description to the people who were supposed to pick me up so that when I got off the plane they would recognize me.

Well, the man who went in my place is about the same height, but he weighs about 90 pounds dripping wet. Also, he has dark, short hair, no beard, and no mustache. When he walked up to the person holding the Don Nori sign, the guy looked at him, and said, "Well, you're not the person we're here to get."

"Well, I know I'm not the person, because he couldn't come."

"Well, we were told to pick up a guy with gray hair, a ponytail, and who weighs about 160 pounds; you only weigh 90 pounds; we know who we're supposed to pick up, and you're not that person."

And so these guys had a real dilemma. They had a written description of the guy they were supposed to meet at the airport, but the person who actually showed up did not fit the description. Now they could have left my assistant sitting in the airport, but they crumpled up the old description and said, "Let's go."

Similarly, we have a description; we think we know who God is; we think we know how He acts—then He shows up with a completely different outfit on, and so we rebuke Him in the name of Jesus. We left the Guy sitting in the airport, or the church, or the living room, when all along it's God. We have to be willing to let our pea brains adjust whenever the God of the universe, who lived from eternity past and will live to eternity future comes alongside us. Here I am with this puny pea brain on this earth 50 years, and *I'm* going to determine what His Presence is like? No, that's not my job, and it scares me a bit to think I would even consider doing that.

He can do whatever He wants to do, and He never violates His Word. However, he will violate what I believe every single day of the week. He is not bound to my erroneous thinking. My decision is whether I'm going to accept reality or whether I am going to cling to a theology that's never proven, manifest, or seen.

TONGUE-TALKIN'

We had meetings at Shippensburg University. A man attended who was a student there; he was crippled with debilitating arthritis. His legs, arms, and back were twisted, and he could barely hold a conversation because of the way his mouth and his face were disfigured by the disease.

This guy turned out to be a "fighting fundie,"—a fighting fundamentalist who serves the great silent God, a God who doesn't talk or do much of anything anymore. I don't know how this man ended up at one of our services, but the Spirit of the Lord was present for healing. We walked back to him, and I put my hand right on his chest—in about 15 seconds he was totally healed. He got up shouting and praising God. He had never been whole in his memory—he had been suffering with the disease since he was a youngster. It was the most awesome thing that had ever happened.

His healing happened on a Monday night, and on Tuesday and Wednesday, he was all over campus telling everybody the big news. Because of his healing, people were flocking to our dormitory, and about 100 students came to the Lord just because of that miracle that God performed.

The following Sunday morning he went strutting into church: "Hey, Pastor, look at me, look!"

The pastor looked at him, totally horrified. "What happened to you?"

"Well, them tongue-talkin' Pentecostals prayed for me, and I got healed. You said that couldn't happen."

The pastor says, "It can't; if you got healed the devil healed you."

So he dragged that young man into his office, and one hour later he had repented for letting us lay hands on him—by the end of the day, he was all shriveled up and crippled again. That incident happened about 10 or 12 years ago, and I still see him shuffling up and down the street. His suffering is getting worse; he can't even shave anymore—what an incredibly sad story.

But this is what happens whenever we don't allow ourselves to hear and respond to the things that God is saying to us. We can always say, "Tsk, tsk, isn't that terrible," and it *is* terrible. But *we* resist those same blessings every day. All of us resist them in different ways, especially when we reach the edge of our comfort zone.

We tend to resist anything beyond our comfort zone as heresy or demonic. That is the point of our repentance. We turn away from our narrow thinking and allow the Holy Spirit to teach us. I don't care what other sin you commit; the sin that prevents you from going farther in your life is the sin of unbelief. You will not believe God can do more than you think He can do. If you think He can't, or won't, take you farther than you already are, then you won't go farther. That is the sin that prevents you from going forward in the purposes of God. I don't care if you lust; I don't care if you drink; I don't care if you lie, slander, or gossip; the sin that's going to prevent you from reaching your God-given destiny is unbelief.

This type of unbelief kept Israel from moving forward and entering the Promised Land. They did not fulfill their destiny; the generation could not move into what God had destined for them because of their unbelief. They would not let their faith go beyond what they had determined was right, and then their flesh, ego, and pride killed them; they would not let God do any more, and they found themselves stopped short of His glory.

And yet the Scriptures say, *"Be careful that none of you fall short of the glory of God"* (see Rom. 3:23).

OUR PROMISED LAND

The children of Israel were in an incredible situation, much like the one we find ourselves in sometimes. They lived in the midst of miracles in the wilderness. He provided them fresh bread every morning. They had fresh water 24 hours a day, and they had quail to eat. Their clothes and shoes grew with them and never wore out. They had a flame by night to keep them warm, and the cloud by day to keep them cool. They were living in the miraculous of God, and yet God was not pleased with them because they would not let Him take them beyond their comfort zone.

They limited themselves by saying, This is what we believe; that's all we believe, and anything else is from the pit. They, more or less, stuck their feet in the sand and told God, "This is all the farther we're going." Consequently, they missed the very thing they were born to fulfill.

We can be just as stubborn. We come out of Egypt to go into the Promised Land, but when things get a little "out there" for us, we stop and stick our feet into the carpet and think, *I'm not going any farther— it's getting too uncomfortable.* But He didn't take us out this far, the Scripture says, to take us back again. He brought us out of bondage to take us into the Promised Land. Yet it's our unbelief that causes us to fall short of the glory of God.

You might say, "But, Nori, you're all wet. I experience the miraculous of God all the time, God answers my prayers; He supplies all my needs; He gives me everything I want. Now you're telling me that I'm falling short of the glory of God?"

That's right. That's what I'm saying.

Israel got everything they wanted; Israel had every need taken care of, but the Scripture says, "God was not pleased" (see 1 Cor. 10:1-4). He took care of them; why? Because they were His. God takes care of you because you belong to Him. But if you're going to touch your destiny, you must say yes to Him beyond your place of comfort, beyond your place of ego, beyond your place of greatest resistance.

Don't let the trickster get you to believe that just because you are experiencing the miraculous, there is no more. Remember, the miracles were intended to help the children of Israel move into a new land, a new way of living, a deeper relationship with their Lord. They looked awesome, mighty, powerful to the rest of the world, but they themselves could not understand what God had for them. He had prepared for them a place of rest and peace and intimate relationship.

We, too, know how to look spiritual; we know how to walk, act, and sound spiritual; we know what television shows to watch—and we know what shows not to tell anybody we watch. We know what movies to go to, and what movies to wait to watch on DVD. We just know how to "look" spiritual.

But deep inside each of us, there is a wall of resistance that we do not want to go beyond because of our unbelief. We think, *I just can't accept that; I just can't do it. What am I going to leave behind?*

Remember, it's easy to leave Egypt because you leave the sin you hate, *but* it's hard to leave the wilderness because you have to leave the sin you crave. The thing within us that prevents us from going forward is the thing that we do not want to change; we don't want to give it up; we *need* it.

In a sense, as in J.R.R. Tolkien's *The Lord of the Rings,* we have a ring, and we are the lord of it—we hold it close to us and say, "precious, precious." It obscures our vision, it threatens our peace, and it turns us from gentle believers into mean, nasty people who keep hold of that "precious thing" that nobody else knows about. But God knows.

HIS BLOOD

There is a penetration of the Spirit of God that needs to occur in us that will make us willing to say "yes" to Him. Penetrating the wall cannot happen except in one place—the Most Holy Place and the manifest presence of God. He alone has the power to change our thoughts, our minds, and our desires.

He alone puts His truth against my lie, His life against my religious resistance, His compassion against my flapping tongue that slanders, lies, and tears down people, pastors, and relationships. Only the manifest presence of God can shut up that tongue. Only the manifest presence of God can turn my faithlessness into faithfulness.

God's desire is to help us get to the place where we will say "yes" to Him. Where we will simply say "yes, you can change me; you can have me; you can do with me what you want to do." The joy of the Lord is in the manifest presence of God. The joy of the Lord is in the *yes* of God. And the blood calls to us, "Come." His blood calls to us.

When Jesus spread the blood, it was sprinkled from the Holy Place to the Most Holy Place, and the blood calls to us, "Come, come, come, come." Remember, His blood covers us until His power delivers us so that we can stand in the presence of God and live. Thank You, Jesus.

The revelation of Christ is an ongoing revelation that constantly draws us to Him. The revelation of Christ is a simple one: you are covered; you are free; the guilt is gone; the shame is gone. You can receive His salvation at high noon, repent at one minute after noon, and at two minutes after noon, listen to God talking to you, telling you what to do.

When Christians discover that they are truly forgiven, the trickster is finished. The lie of guilt and the weight of sin are gone. You are truly free to serve the Lord Jesus.

If you are still struggling with guilt about a past sin, you need to know that the first time you repented, you were forgiven. Somebody should have told you about the power of the blood of Jesus. Somebody should have told you about the mercy and compassion of God. There is no need to carry guilt and shame that cause you to fall short of the glory of God. You will continue to fall short of fulfilling the thing that God called you to do.

If you are living in guilt, you need to know you are forgiven. Second Corinthians 5:18 says that *"God gave us the work of bringing people back to Himself."* When you confess your sins, you can declare you are right with God. If appropriate, pray right now as though you have never been born again, and give Jesus your sin, just as you gave it to Him when you first prayed to Him.

Every time you sin, pray the same way, and the blood of Jesus covers, forgives, and washes you so that you can live without guilt or shame. The world has yet to see what can happen through a forgiven Church, what can happen to the world. Amazing, supernatural, and life-changing things will happen.

What would you be doing right now if you knew you were forgiven? What would be different right now if you knew with your heart, of heart, of heart, of heart, of hearts that you were forgiven? I'm sure your life would change for the better.

It is the accuser of the brethren—the trickster—who keeps us in guilt and shame. The enemy comes to kill, steal, and destroy. When you confess your sins to Jesus, they are thrown into the "depths of the sea" (Micah 7:19 NASB). As far as the east is from the west is how far He separates you from your sin (see Ps. 103:12). *"Your sins are red like deep red cloth,"* the Scripture says, *"But they can be as white as snow"* (Isa. 1:18).

When you sin on Monday and ask Jesus to forgive you, He forgives you on Monday. Then on Tuesday when you say, "Lord, I did it again." Very honestly the Lord says to you, "Did what again?" Because your sin is in the sea of forgetfulness, He chooses not to count your sin against you; He chooses not to remember your sin.

So if you remember your sin, who's reminding you? If you remember what you did, who are you listening to? If you think, *I never hear anything from the supernatural,* you are wrong. If you are feeling guilty for a God-forgiven sin, you are hearing the devil telling you you're guilty. Stop listening to him!

When God tells us something, we can believe it as truth. When you look in the mirror and God says, "Thou woman of faith, I will use you beyond what you can imagine." You might say, "Lord, can you confirm that to me, please." So that night after a really bad day, we look in the mirror again, and the devil says, "You are such a jerk." And we say, "Oh, yeah, you're right." That's *not* the way our mirror talk should go.

When God tells us something, we think that He needs to confirm it five ways before we can believe it. But when the devil tells us something, we believe it right away. See how backward, how very backward, our theology is? Why are we taught that? Why do we believe that? Why do we believe the worst about ourselves? Our religious ways of thinking keep us under the thumb of control and tradition. This system is not the Church Jesus is building.

The world is yet to see the Church that really believes it is forgiven. This is the Church of the third day, the Church of the Most Holy Place. The word that proceeds from the mouth of God goes straight to our hearts, piercing our innermost being, and we must say yes.

When the flesh tries to tell us lies, we can slap them down. When the enemy tries to tell you lies, slap him down. Lies remind you of sin long ago forgiven. A surefire way to know if you really believe that your sin is forgiven is for the devil to remind you of it. If you believe that God has forgiven you, you can respond to satan's reminder in this way: "In fact, I do remember that sin. Thank You, Jesus, for forgiving me for that; that was awesome. Thank You, Lord."

Let's change the way we think; let's be transformed by the renewing of our minds; let's allow Jesus to talk to us, encourage us, bless us, and draw us to Himself. Let's rediscover our first love and the freedom of our salvation experience by taking time to pray:

Prayer Pause: *"Lord Jesus, I need You. I know that I'm a sinner. I know that I fall short of Your glory. I believe You are the Son of God. I believe You shed your blood for my sins. I believe Your blood can cover me, forgive me, and cleanse me. Lord Jesus, I ask You to forgive me, a sinner; I ask You to come into my heart to live and rule there. Forgive me, and stay with me forever, for I accept Your forgiveness. Cover me with Your blood, in Jesus' Name, amen."*

I declare you reconciled to God. And what God has joined together, let no devil tear asunder. Hallelujah. Don't allow the enemy to get to you through your "human nature" and take your peace and freedom away from you anymore, ever.

> *Why does the robber come? Only to steal, kill, and destroy. I came, so that they might have life—to the fullest!* (John 10:10)

If the enemy can influence us in any way, you can be certain that he will try. This is what you need to know. He will pluck the Word from your heart, or he will sow "word seeds" that will result in doubt, confusion, depression, or just plain frustration. All he needs to do is sidetrack you from the Lord, and he has done his job. Your commission, therefore, is this:

> *Be alert! Watch! The Devil is your enemy. He is like a lion. He walks around, roaring and looking for someone to eat* (1 Peter 5:8).

> *Pray with the Spirit at all times. Use all kinds of prayers and requests. Be on guard! Always pray for all the holy people* (Ephesians 6:18).

Chapter 7

THE NATURE OF HUMANKIND

How many people truly understand what is inside just one person? Only that person's spirit really knows. In the same way, only the spirit of God knows all about God (1 Corinthians 2:11).

God's message is alive and active. It is sharper than any sword with two sharp edges. It can slice between the soul and the spirit or between the joints and bone marrow. It can tell the difference between the desires and the intentions of the human mind (Hebrews 4:12).

HUMANKIND AND THE TEMPLE OF GOD

To understand how the trickster infiltrates our humanity, it is important to know the correlation between the body, His corporate Body the Church, and the supernatural reality of His Temple, which is you. Yes, because you have enormous ability to hear and participate in the supernatural activity of the Holy Spirit as a daily experience.

You yourselves know that you are God's temple sanctuary. Don't you know that the Spirit of God lives in you? (1 Corinthians 3:16).

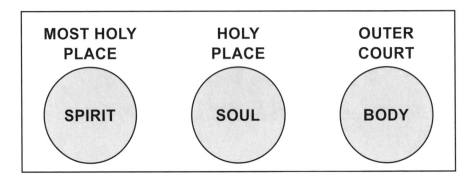

The body is like the outer court—it is outside, and its life is seen by all. It is here that man obeys God's commands. It is here that Christ died in the flesh on display for all to see.

The soul is like the holy place—it is on display for all to see. It is the place of duality. Here is the battleground of life. Who will you listen to?

The spirit is like the Most Holy Place, the secret place of the Most High God. The only light is the light of His glory. Here man communicates with God. The work of the temple is determined by what happens in the Most Holy Place. The revelations in that place determine the work of the temple…and so it is with man!

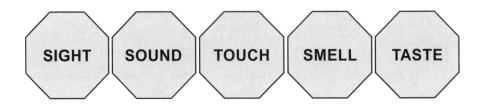

BODY—WORLD CONSCIOUSNESS

There are five *senses* in the body of man that allow him to interface and communicate with the physical world…sight, sound, touch, smell, and taste. We live in a time when great emphasis is placed on the body. *Fanaticism on health, athleticism, and beauty try to enforce a focus on the things that fade away. Although care of the body is critical, obsessive focus on the body sidetracks us from eternal issues.*

The older you become, the more in tune you become with your physical body, and you begin to realize that this body is passing away no matter what you do. By then, it is often too late. It is better to learn to take care of the body because it is the Temple of the Lord, not because we are in a beauty contest.

SOUL—SELF CONSCIOUSNESS

The will is the deliberating organ; it is the power of making judgment. Decisions are made here, a critical part of God's working in man.

The mind is the thinking organ; it is the processing part of the soul. Our intelligence, knowledge, and everything that has to with our mental capacity comes from the mind.

The emotions are the feeling organ; it is the affective part of man. Love, hatred, anger, jealousy, passion, sorrow, and happiness come from the emotive part of the soul.

Man's thoughts, imaginations, judgments, feelings, emotions, stimulations, and desires arise out of man's soul.

Emotions also are evident as we respond to the spirit. Because emotions are in the soul, they will be expressed from stimuli coming from any dimension.

The soul is the true "I," the self, the ego of man. It is in this realm that the raw data of the body and spirit is delivered, analyzed, and studied. It is where final decisions are made based on the information gathered by these two areas.

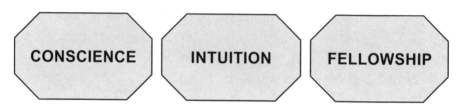

SPIRIT—GOD CONSCIOUSNESS

The conscience is the discerning organ; it is the part that renders judgment on right and wrong. It is a spontaneous and direct judgment that is not influenced by the knowledge of the mind. Your mind can say it is right, but the conscience has the final word.

Intuition is the revealing organ; it is the part that provides light for the spirit. The intuitive part of the spirit does not need the knowledge of the soul. The intuitive part of the spirit provides supernatural knowledge (i.e., word of knowledge, word of wisdom, discerning of spirits). All of God's revelation is revealed in the spirit of man. It is here where man truly knows God and His mysteries.

But as you grow in the Lord, you will discover that the gift you are currently flowing in is unimportant. You will be relying upon the Lord Jesus, who indwells you in all His fullness. No wonder Paul said, *"I can do anything—by the one who gives me the power"* (Phil. 4:13).

God is in Jesus, and Jesus is in us. Therefore, God is in me. Here is one of the prayers Paul prayed for you and me:

...to know the love of Christ which surpasses knowledge, that you may be filled up to all the fullness of God. Now to Him who is able to do exceeding abundantly beyond all that we ask or think, according to the power that works within us (Ephesians 3:19-20 NASB).

The focus of our spiritual development must be in the spirit realm. The whole picture of our existence is locked in this most misunderstood realm, for in this realm our purpose and place in the universe will be discovered and ultimately understood.

The more we give ourselves to the Lord in order to discover the vastness of Him and the cosmos in which we dwell, the more we will grow as spiritual people and as human beings. This focus will open to us the high calling of humanity, the incredible love that created us, and the supreme confidence God has in mere humanity filled up with Him. The more we give ourselves to the wanton desires of the fleshly side of humanity, the more we will grow dark in spirit. This focus will actually strengthen the fleshly cravings of unregenerate man, making it more difficult to respond to the Holy Spirit.

These are not the elementary thoughts of a religion, but the rudimentary truths of our existence. Religion cannot fathom this existence. Philosophy will never understand it, and theology can never explain it. It eludes the intellectual who is focused exclusively on either one realm or another. The truth lies in the marriage of regenerate man and the Spirit of God. It is in this incredible union that the earth is freed from the bondage and ravages of earthly humanity, as the sons of God, broken of heart but strengthened in resolve, begin to redeem the world with the unconditional love of God. This is why Jesus came. This is why He was raised from the dead. This is why He lives in the hearts of those who trust Him with their salvation. This is how He will fill the earth with His glory. He will use unlikely people like you and me.

This dual consciousness will present us a full picture, or as full a picture as we can expect, of life the way God intended it to be. As I have presented earlier, we are often so bound by the limitations of the natural mind that is trained to resist all things intangible, that we miss the greatest adventures yet ahead of us as a race, as spiritual people, and as believers in the Redeemer.

TRUE DISCERNMENT

Discernment also fades when we choose the fleshly side of man. Things become confused, undistinguishable. However, discernment becomes sharp and keen when we give ourselves to the "higher" calling of God in Spirit and the "higher" call of our original creation. The trickster will rule freely when we are unwilling to see into the realm of spirit. He will keep us confused and impotent as long as we allow ourselves to be ruled by the limitations of the five senses.

> *And so, the little boy was growing up and becoming stronger in spirit. John lived in the desert, away from other people, until the time when he came out to preach to Israel* (Luke 1:80).

> *The way human nature thinks is death, but the way the Spirit thinks is life and peace* (Romans 8:6).

The soul's direction of focus needs to be toward the spirit. It needs to look to the spirit for its development. We must remember that we are constantly body-conscious. We are aware of all things natural, but few things spiritual. To expand our wisdom and knowledge, to have a greater ability to discern the truth in a matter, we must develop our ability to focus on the Holy Spirit and begin receiving at least as much data from this realm as we do from the five senses.

Here, the need to be in true spiritual worship cannot be overemphasized. We need to discover and learn to be at home with His Presence. In worship, we learn the sense of His Presence and the wonder of His realm of spirit that holds such power and promise for us. True spiritual worship is not three songs tucked between the welcome and the offering; it is a sustained time of personal and corporate worship and adoration to our Lord and God. It is a time of yielding, giving, and heartfelt thankfulness for all He has done. In this environment, we learn the sense of His Presence and benefit from the healing power His Presence always brings.

DISCOVERING THE REALITY OF HIS PRESENCE

Soon after I discovered how much Jesus loved me, I went through an awful situation. It was the first major test of my walk with God. I was so young, so ignorant, and in many ways, so alone. But during this time, I had a weight in my spirit that I had not known and certainly did not understand. It was frightening. It was with me continuously. I slept to try to get away from it, but as soon as I would awaken, it was there again. But the trouble passed, and so did this weight on my spirit.

It was a few years later that I discovered the glory of true spiritual worship. To my shock and surprise, the worship brought on this same sense that I had happily left behind a few years earlier. Every time I worshiped, this feeling came over me. I could not get away from it. After several months of this, I made a wonderful discovery. The weight I was feeling was the Presence of the Lord. I realized then that He was with me during that most trying time a few years before. I spent several days in tearful gratitude for His Presence during that time. I did not realize He was with me; I actually felt as though He had abandoned me. But once I understood His presence, I knew He was with me the entire time. I was never alone. Oh, how critical it is to learn His Presence! How comforting to recognize His nearness and His comfort. My life would never be the same, all because I learned the sense of His Presence!

THE POWER OF VISION OVER THE TRICKSTER

Most of us do not understand how powerful our vision is.

> *One time, I went to the house of Shemaiah, the son of Dela-iah. Delaiah was the son of Mehetabel....He said, "Let us meet together in the house of God—inside the temple—and close the doors of the temple. Men are coming to kill you! Men will come at night to kill you!"* (Nehemiah 6:10)

Words of comfort often come from those who seem to want to help and encourage us, but we always need a spirit of discernment to know the difference from those who are deceiving us and those who have our best interest in their hearts.

Vision is stronger than a man's words.

> *I recognized that God had not sent him. Tobiah and San-ballat had paid him some money to speak such a prophecy against me. They had hired Shemaiah to try to scare me. They wanted me to enter the temple, which would be a sin. Then they could destroy my good name. They wanted to discredit me* (Nehemiah 6:12-13).

Discernment is essential if we are to serve the Lord in the face of opposition.

People with true vision and direction are a threat:

1. They threaten those who have no reason to live.

2. They threaten those whose vision is contrary to the purposes of the Lord.

3. They threaten the system.

OUR NATURE

Humans love externals. We love to be told what to do, and when to do it. That is why the Old Covenant is so enticing. But in Christ, everything is not as it appears; often, it is backward from the way the world sees life.

In Christ,

- To win you must be last.

- To be rich you must give everything away.

- To be seen of God you must hide from others.

- To be promoted you must promote others.

- To gain favor you must cease your labors.

- To be strong you must be weak.

- To live you must die.

- To lead you must serve.

The trickster will always tempt you to yearn for the top, the best, the first, the most prestigious, the most powerful. But in Christ, the servant is at the top. The one who dies is the most powerful. The richest are the ones who give everything away.

REMEMBER WHO YOU ARE!

Every time I write about faith, it seems that I should reassure you that God loves you and really wants to bless you.

How many times have you said or heard others say, "Why have faith? I am too messed up for Him to bless me."

But His Word says:

Who may go up to the mountain of the Always-Present One? Who is allowed to stand in His holy temple? Only those with clean hands and pure hearts. One who has not worshiped idols. One must not have sworn vows by a false god. This is the one who will receive a blessing from the Always-Present One. The God who saves such a person will declare him to be righteous. This person tries to follow God. They look to the God of Jacob for help. (Selah) (Psalm 24:3-6).

Jacob? Why Jacob? Why not Abraham or Isaac or Noah? Jacob could not save himself. He was a thief from his birth. But God loved him. God forgave him. There was no reason that God should favor Jacob; He just did. Likewise, you and I are loved, forgiven, and blessed just because He wanted to, just because He did. We did nothing to get it; we can do nothing to take it away. He loves us, forgives, heals us, lavishes His mercy and grace upon us, and calls us by His Name. We are what we are…children of God.

We are born of Jacob—the one who does not deserve God's love but gets it anyway. God loves, forgives, and cleanses Jacob—and us. The God of Jacob does not disqualify us. He forgives us and encourages us to go on.

Don't put your trust in princes or in any other human being. None of them can save you. When they die, they are buried. On that day, all of their plans perish. Happy is the one who gets help from the God of Jacob. His hope is in the Always-Present One, his God. He made heaven and earth, the sea and everything in it. He remains loyal forever. He does what is fair for those who have been wronged. He gives food to the hungry people. The Always-Present One sets the prisoners free. The Always-Present One gives sight to the blind people. The Always-Present One lifts up people who are in trouble. The Always-Present One loves those who do right. The Always-Present One protects the foreigners. He helps the widows and orphans. But He frustrates the plans of the evil people (Psalm 146:3-9).

We live by believing, not by seeing (2 Corinthians 5:7).

Let the peace of Christ direct your hearts. God called you in one body to peace. Be thankful. Let the teaching of Christ live among you in an abundant way. Use all wisdom to teach and warn one another with psalms, songs of praise, and spiritual songs, singing to God with your hearts. Everything you say or do should be done by the authority of the Lord Jesus. Thank God the Father through Christ (Colossians 3:15-17).

Whatever you do, work at it—really hard—as if it were for the Lord, not men. Be a slave to Christ, the master. You know you will receive a reward from the Lord; it will be an inheritance (Colossians 3:23-24).

Faith gives us the ability to allow the free flow between the natural and the spiritual. Faith moves us into the spirit and moves the spiritual from eternity into time and space. Everything God is and does is spiritual. His existence is in the dimension of spirit. Our faith moves what is in this dimension into the realm that we live in.

FAITH WORKS IN TWO DIRECTIONS

1. Faith is the part of us that reaches into the spiritual to receive all God has promised for us. This action of faith takes care of the physical part of us so we can respond to the Spirit.

2. Faith is also the part of us that allows us to live in the Spirit, see in the Spirit, and move in the Spirit. This action of faith allows us to dwell where He is and function in the spirit realm.

*Faith is the title-deed to the things we hope for. Faith is being sure of things we cannot see. The elders had this kind of faith long ago. It pleased God. By faith, we understand that the universe was put together by God's word. What we see was made from what we cannot see. By faith, Abel offered God a better sacrifice than Cain did. Abel was a good man, through faith. God was pleased with his gifts. Abel is dead, but, through faith, he still speaks to us. By faith, Enoch was taken up to God. He did not die: "No one could find Enoch because God had taken him to heaven." Before Enoch was taken up, it was said that he pleased God. If someone doesn't believe in God, he cannot please God, because the person who comes to God **must** believe that He lives. That person must also believe that God will give rewards to the people who are searching for Him* (Hebrews 11:1-6).

Faith is the energy that causes the interaction between God and humankind. Faith causes us to move outside ourselves and embrace what is not seen by the human eye. God intends this to be our lifestyle.

Faith can move in us and through us every moment of every day. Faith causes us to move…to do something…to respond to faith.

By faith, when God warned Noah about some future things which could not be seen yet, Noah built a ship to save his family. He respected God. Through his faith, Noah showed that the world was wrong. He received the kind of righteousness that comes from faith. By faith, when God called Abraham to go away to a place that he would later receive as an inheritance, Abraham obeyed. He left, not knowing where he was going. By faith, Abraham lived as a foreigner in the promised land. He lived in tents. Isaac and Jacob did too. They were to receive the same promise from God (Hebrews 11:7-9).

By faith even Sarah herself received ability to conceive, even beyond the proper time of life, since she considered Him faithful who had promised (Hebrews 11:11 NASB).

By faith, when God tested Abraham, Abraham offered Isaac as a sacrifice (Hebrews 11:17).

By faith, Isaac talked about sure things when he blessed Jacob and Esau. By faith, when Jacob was dying, he blessed both of Joseph's sons. Jacob "worshiped, leaning on the top of his walking cane." By faith, when Joseph was near death, he remembered that God said that the sons of Israel would leave Egypt. And he gave orders about burying his bones. By faith, after Moses was born, his parents hid him for three months. They were not afraid to disobey the king's order. They saw that he was no ordinary baby. By faith, when Moses had grown up, he said no to being called "Pharaoh's daughter's son" (Hebrews 11:20-24).

Today, we are going to release our faith to believe God for the interaction between man and God and what He wants for us. He loves us.

He will give us discernment and understanding into the depth of His plan for us.

Chapter 8

SEE WHAT YOU HAVE NEVER SEEN

About the Message of life: What has existed since the beginning we heard, we saw with our own eyes, we watched, we touched with our hands....Now to you also we are telling the things we have seen and heard... (1 John 1:1-3).

T HERE IS A DEPTH OF REALITY, a depth of existence that will change us completely once we understand it. As mentioned previously, we are spiritual people. We are meant to live in and experience the Lord in spirit realm—more specifically, in the Holy Spirit, who exists in the spirit realm. The experience we have with the Lord in the Spirit is then lived out in the natural world.

John expressed this when he wrote,

In the beginning was the Word, and the Word was with God, and the Word was God. The Word became human and lived among us for a while. We saw His glory, the kind of glory like that of the Father's one and only Son—full of gracious love and truth (John 1:1,14).

Because God is Spirit, He dwells in every dimension. We, too, can experience life in the Spirit and in this natural realm.

To live in the *Spirit* is different from living in the spirit realm. For instance, I have many friends in Pescara, Italy, but I have to know their street addresses so I can visit them. Simply to be in the city of Pescara does not mean I am with my friends. I may be in the correct city, but unless I am at the right address, I cannot expect the welcome and hospitality that I enjoy when I am with them.

Many people live in the spirit realm, but do not have the peace and safety of living in the Holy Spirit. They wander in this realm of spirit without the guidance and protection of the Holy Spirit. They will listen to any voice they hear, respond to anything that passes their way. They will converse with these spirits without knowing who they are or what their intentions may be. This, as you can imagine, is dangerous, indeed. There are many who can be in touch with the spirit realm, but the believer has the added advantage of being in Christ. The Scriptures never refute the existence of ghosts or any other kind of spirit. The only spirit that can be trusted implicitly, however, is the Holy Spirit. We must learn to recognize and respond to Him. As you have discovered thus far, this is not a difficult assignment as He is as recognizable as one of your best friends.

God wants us to be truly discerning, to be able to understand the natural as well as the spiritual input we get. Then our decisions can be informed decisions. We must be careful, though, or our emotions will overwhelm what the Holy Spirit is trying to show us. It is not enough to have earthly wisdom. Listen to what Jesus said about discernment: "...*You can understand changes in the sky which show a change in the weather, but you cannot understand the signs of change of this time in history*" (Matt. 16:3).

Discernment is a strong weapon against the lies we believe. Paul encourages us to grow in this discernment:

This is what I am praying for: I want your love to overflow more and more with a fuller knowledge and all insight. Then you will be able to test what is best, so you will be pure and without guilt when Christ comes. You will be filled with what righteousness produces through Jesus Christ for the glory and praise of God (Philippians 1:9-11).

True worship increases discernment. When you perceive what is real, you can sense what is fake. When you know the ways of God, the lies of the enemy will be easier to detect and respond to. It is interesting that the U.S. government trains its law enforcement agents by teaching them how to recognize the truth. They do not spend so much time on studying the counterfeit. The government knows that the best defense against counterfeit money is knowing how to recognize the genuine.

AN URGENCY

We hear all over the world about how the Holy Spirit is moving anew and afresh. But we also hear how there is opposition to this movement. It is important that we understand the difference between what God wants to do and what man wants to do. God will do what He wants to do without our permission. He does not need to ask our opinion. He only asks our cooperation.

When something unusual happens, it is important that the people have a discerning spirit to know what is from the Lord. The church that will change the world in these last days is the church that will be able to hear from the Lord. We alone carry the responsibility for the Word of the Lord to our hearts. We must have a spirit that can touch the Spirit of God. We must have a spirit that can discern what is happening in the spirit realm.

Although we live in the Holy Spirit, which is within the spirit realm, we should be able to discern the entire spirit realm, anywhere in the world.

The months and the years ahead are going to be extremely challenging. We are going to need God's Presence and power more than we have ever needed it before. The level of power we have had in the past will not withstand the onslaught the enemy will launch against us. But God's power is not the problem. He will send as much power as we need to overcome the enemy. The problem is never God's power; the problem is our ability to allow God to show Himself in new ways. The problem is our ability to say yes to the Lord even when it goes against the traditions we have experienced.

God will have disciples in this generation who will not allow themselves to be persuaded by the words of man, but by the spirit of discernment in their hearts.

I have an urgency in my spirit about how important it is to be able to discern the lies of the enemy. God wants our hearts open and ready so that whenever He does what He is about to do, there will be people ready to say yes to Him. And while confused men argue amongst themselves in the corner, the army of the living God will rise up and do the will of God.

I am not interested in the arguments of man anymore. Jesus says that we will know His disciples by their fruit (see Matt. 7:20). The Word says that every good tree bears good fruit, but bad trees bear bad fruit (see Matt. 7:17). A good tree can't produce bad fruit any more than a bad tree can produce good fruit. In other words, Jesus is saying, "Don't look at what they say; look at what they are producing." Anybody can sit in the seat of the scornful and criticize and rebuke and find fault. But it takes men and women of courage who will not listen to those voices but instead will give themselves to the Spirit of the Lord and examine the fruit to determine the will of God and His activity.

Paul demonstrated God's *power*, not words. In First Corinthians 2:4-5, Paul says, *"...I preached the message. I showed that it was backed up by the Spirit and real power. Why? So that your trust would not depend upon human wisdom, but upon God's power!"* He goes on to say,

We are speaking true wisdom to people who are spiritually mature. We are not talking about what this world calls "wisdom" or the rulers of this world, who are losing their power. No, we are talking about God's secret wisdom, which has been hidden. Since before time began, God planned this glory for us. None of the rulers of this world understood this. If they had known it, they would not have nailed the Lord of glory to the cross. This has been written: "No eye has ever seen this and no ear has ever heard this. No human being has ever imagined this. But this is what God prepared for those who love Him" (1 Corinthians 2:6-9).

CHANGE YOUR WORLD

If there are things we have not seen, if there are things we have not heard, if there are things that have never entered into our hearts before, then they are new things to us. They are things we have not experienced previously. If we are going to move forward and mature in the things God wants for us in His Kingdom here and now, we have to trust Him concerning the new things we will experience.

God does not live in a box. We do not live in a box; we do not live in a sealed room. In fact, the Bible says that we, like Abraham, are looking for a city made without hands whose builder and maker is God (see Heb. 11:9-10). We are looking for a city we have not seen before. We are looking for the love of God in ways we have never before experienced!

If we keep doing what we have always done, we will always get what we always have had. I don't know about you, but I am not satisfied with what I have always had. Are you satisfied that there are only about 50 to 100 people in each church? Are you satisfied that there are so few people healed? Although we may not be satisfied, we continue to go through the same rituals week after week. We sing the same songs, preach the same sermons, repeat the same special services over and over. Nothing improves. Nothing changes. We live far below the *"glory to glory"* the Scriptures talk about (see 2 Cor. 3:18).

I challenge you to become a person of discernment. I challenge you to seek Him like you have never sought the Lord before so that you may begin to discern the things that are God and the things that are not God. Listen to what the apostle John says: *"These things I have written to you concerning those who are trying to deceive you"* (1 John 2:26 NASB).

The Lord does not want you to be deceived. He doesn't want you to be overpowered by the words of others and of the trickster who try to convince us with human reason and outright lies.

> *God gave you a gift. You still have this gift inside you. You don't need anyone to teach you. The gift that He gave you teaches you about everything. This gift is true; it is not false. Because of this, continue to live in God, just as His gift taught you* (1 John 2:27).

This is a verse we don't have to be afraid of; it does not mean we do not need teachers. It means there is a spirit of understanding that dwells in each one of us; the witness of God's Spirit should flourish in our hearts. And that Witness flourishing within us is teaching us right from wrong. The best thing we can do for our children, for example, is to teach them the Spirit of discernment. Teach them the truth that the Presence of the Lord abides within them.

Do you remember when Mary went to visit Elizabeth? As soon as Elizabeth heard the voice of Mary, the babe leapt within her (see Luke 1:41). The Spirit of discernment is just like that. Because His Presence abides within us, every time we hear something that is from the Holy Spirit, the babe leaps within us, so to speak. The Holy Spirit says *yes*, and we know we have heard from the Lord. Conversely, when something evil is said, the Presence within responds quite differently. We feel a hesitation, an inner warning that should cause us to proceed very cautiously. The anointing within us teaches us.

GOD IN A BOX

Now there are times when we need to teach; there is a time for everything, but over the past several hundred years we have made no time for Him. We have made time for our preaching; we have made time for our order of worship; but we have made no time for Him. The Lord is going to take His Church back to Himself. Jesus said, *"I will build my community—those called out by God. Death will not overpower them"* (Matt. 16:18). So I believe that pastors need to be the assistant pastor to Jesus. We just need to do what He says to do. In fact, He is the One who started this way of "preaching." He is the One who said that "whatever I see my Father in Heaven doing, that is what I will do. If I don't see my Father in Heaven doing it, I ain't doin' it!" (my paraphrase). The actual verse says it this way:

> I am telling you the truth: The Son can do nothing on His own. He can only do what He sees the Father doing. Whatever the Father may do, the Son will do the same thing (John 5:19).

Do you remember when Jesus was at the pool of Bethesda? There were hundreds of sick people there, but Jesus only saw His Father healing one. That's the only one He healed, and then He walked away from the pool of Bethesda, leaving hundreds of sick people. Why did He do that? I have no idea. He is God, and He does what He wants to do. He wants followers who will love Him enough to do *only* what He says to do.

THE ENEMY LIMITS WHAT GOD CAN DO

You must be careful when someone says, "God didn't, can't, won't, hasn't"—or anything that limits God. He is an ever-expanding God. He is as big as He will ever be, but our understanding of Him should expand over time. We must allow ourselves to be challenged and changed as we see more of His life in the Word and in our experience.

We must step out of the way and let Him do what He wants to do. We must be strong enough in our spirits and mature enough in our hearts to discern the work of the Holy Spirit and to let His Spirit flow.

There will be men and women who will stand firm and say, "Wait, we will not let you limit God like that anymore; we have seen Him, and we have heard Him." The apostle John said that which we have seen and heard and handled of the good Word; this is what we declare to you (see 1 John 1:1-3). We don't declare theory. We don't declare theology. His disciples will rise up and once and for all silence those who are resisting the Holy Spirit, who are allowing themselves to be used by satan to limit the work of God in the land.

DISCERNMENT GROWS IN HIS PEOPLE

Discernment is received in a very simple way. Discernment grows in us in correlation with the time we spend with our minds toward the Lord and in His Presence. The more time you spend in God's Presence, the more discernment you have.

I mentioned earlier that I had trouble discerning the times and seasons of things I saw in the spirit, since everything is now in that dimension of timelessness. Over the years, I had to learn to not only hear, but to ask when these things should take place. This growth helps me to be a better businessman, father, and prophet.

As to this salvation, the prophets who prophesied of the grace that would come to you made careful search and inquiry, seeking to know what person or time the Spirit of Christ within them was indicating as He predicted the sufferings of Christ and the glories to follow (1 Peter 1:10-11 NASB).

You learn how His Presence moves and how He thinks. Consequently, life in His Presence and in worship becomes a very important part of your life. As you learn how His Presence feels, you discover how He responds to circumstances, just as we discussed in an earlier chapter.

The world and its religious system want you to believe your five senses more than the Holy Spirit. The religious system wants you to trust reason more than His presence or the name of Jesus.

But the Lord wants followers who will grow in discernment and who will have the courage to stand up against the trickster. You know what is right. You know what you have experienced. You know how God has touched you. For you there is no argument. You must make your stand. I pray that you will grow in discernment and together we will stop acting like mere mortals and start acting like the spiritual men and women we really are. God made us in His image. In Jesus' name we need to commit ourselves to being spiritual people.

Chapter 9

DESTROYING THE TRICKSTER'S PLANS

But they have defeated him because of the Lamb's blood and because of the message of their testimony. Even when they were about to die, they did not love their lives more than God (Revelation 12:11).

I T IS DIFFICULT TO BELIEVE that there is real hope for a victory if you are not certain of the provisions for that win. The Scriptures are full of non negotiable facts surrounding the work of Jesus on the Cross. In no uncertain terms, the reality of the resurrection of Jesus from the dead, His defeat of satan, and the Lord's very personal invitation for us to join Him in the Spirit is repeated again and again. He knew that the human race would think it was too good to be true. It is too much for us to believe that Someone would have such a great love for mere humanity that He would sacrifice His Son so they would be free from the grasp of the evil one—only then to be given the free choice to either follow the Lord or not.

Such love seems far too implausible for us. But faith is a wonderful thing! It allows us to reach into the unknown, the unproven, and the unseen to bring to light those things that were hidden so we can see with the eyes of our hearts, and experience, in reality, the wonders of so great a salvation.

Here is just one example, in Paul's words, of what Jesus did and continues to do on behalf of humanity:

> *When you were spiritually dead in your sins and your human nature was not circumcised, God brought you back to life with Christ. He forgave all of our sins. God wiped away the written code with its strict orders. It was negative; it was against us. He took it out of the way. He nailed it to the cross. After God stripped away the power of the rulers and authorities, He showed this openly, using the cross to show His victory over them* (Colossians 2:13-15).

THE BREATH OF LIFE

Before you give yourself totally to Him, your spirit is unable to gather data because it is inoperable, dead. But when Jesus breathes His life into you, your spirit comes alive—you are born again. You were born once from your mother's womb; you are born again by the Spirit. It is no wonder that life seems so new, so exciting, so full. For the first time in your life, you are able to receive from the dimension of spirit. You are no longer praying to the air hoping that He hears you (which He does). But now your relationship changes from a monologue to God into a dialogue with your heavenly Father. The Lord actually moves you from satan's dominion (darkness, void of God) to the dominion of Jesus Christ (light, God Present). Paul puts it this way, *"He rescued us from the power of darkness and moved us into the kingdom of His dear Son"* (Col. 1:13).

I love how the Old Testament prophets were able to see cross-dimensionally, thousands of years into the future, into the time of the redemption of Jesus and further into our day as well. They saw wonderful things about the work of salvation toward humanity. In this remarkable passage, the prophet Isaiah tells us that our struggle to please God will come to an end when the Redeemer, Jesus Christ, comes on the scene, which He did more than 2,000 years ago:

> *Your God says, "Comfort, comfort My people. Speak kindly to the people of Jerusalem. Tell them that their time of service is finished. Tell them that they have paid for their sins. Tell them that the Always-Present One has punished Jerusalem twice for every sin they did"* (Isaiah 40:1-2).

When Isaiah speaks to Jerusalem, he is speaking to all who call on the Lord. Our war is over. Our struggle is ended. We are washed, cleansed, purchased, gathered, and under the shadow of His wings:

> *For You have been my help, And in the shadow of Your wings I sing for joy* (Psalm 63:7 NASB).

Now we can rest from the struggle of trying to please the Lord we love. Now our energy can be put toward discovering our wholeness, our freedom, and the destiny that He planned for us since before time began. We no longer have to struggle with whether or not He loves us, or whether or not He will forgive us. After all, if we do not have the strength or ability to save ourselves, what can we do (who love Him with love undying), to separate ourselves from His forgiving power?

Again, the Scripture tackles this very human, very common tendency to think that every failure means we are no longer gathered to Him.

> *I am sure that nothing will be able to separate us from God's love which is found in Christ Jesus, our Lord—none of these things—death, life, angels, rulers, the present time, the future, powers, heights, or depth!* (Romans 8:38-39)

God is not like us. We cannot impose the attitudes and feelings of humankind onto an eternal, ever-loving God.

EVERYTHING IS NEW

Since the day we heard about you, we haven't stopped praying for you. We ask that you may be filled with the knowledge of what God wants, with all kinds of wisdom and spiritual understanding. We want you to live as if you were worthy of the Lord Jesus. Please Him in every way. Produce the fruit of good deeds. Grow in your knowledge of God. Be strong! Have all the strength of His glorious power. Then you will be able to endure anything. You will learn patience with joy (Colossians 1:9-11).

Sounds pretty awesome, doesn't it? It doesn't sound like God expects you to live a life of worry and fear, but rather to live a life filled with strength and confidence.

O my enemy, don't rejoice over me! If I fall, then I will get up! If I sit in darkness, then the Always-Present One will be a Light for me (Micah 7:8).

The prophet Micah knew the power of God's love and understood His determination to complete all that He had intended for Micah. This same power, love, and determination is also the heart of God toward you. His promise is clear and without reservation or condition, *"...Remember, I will always be with you even until the end of time!"* (Matt. 28:20).

Prayer Pause: *Lord Jesus, Thank You for Your great love toward me. Thank You because Your hand is on my life for good. I believe You. I believe You died for me, and I believe that You rose from the dead. I believe all the promises of forgiveness, love, and a renewed mind. Please help me to see all You have done. You are my Lord. I trust Your words; I trust Your love for me. Amen.*

THE TRICKSTER MUST FLEE

*Listen! I have given you the authority to walk on danger-
ous snakes and scorpions—even more power than the enemy
has. Nothing will ever hurt you! The evil spirits obey you.
This is true, but don't be happy for that reason. Instead be
happy because your names are written in heaven* (Luke
10:19-20).

*We live in this world, but we don't fight like people in this
world. For our fight we are not using weapons which come
from this world. No, our weapons come from God. They are
powerful enough to break down strong forts. We break down
false logic and anything which rises up against what we
know is true about God. We capture every thought to make
it obey Christ* (2 Corinthians 10:3-5).

It is interesting to me that we spend so much time on the actual
process and activity of casting out spirits when the Scriptures give us
a more basic understanding of demonic activity. Of course it is always
easier to blame the devil for the things that give us pause in our daily
Christian experience. But it is clear that the things we have most trouble
with are born of the natural, fleshly part of us that tries to control the
soul to get its selfish desires. The Scripture from Second Corinthians is
a very basic primer on understanding what really controls us.

The trickster, the enemy of your soul, knows your weaknesses and
simply exploits them for his own diabolical purposes. Anything that
distracts us from the purposes of God in our lives will be mercilessly
used against us. Satan's only goal is to distract our consciousness from
the Lord—His love, His compassion, His plan, and everything that
encourages us to be what we are called to be and to do. The more we
are aware of who we are and of the destiny that awaits us, the less we
are distracted at every temptation that comes our way. Distractions are
not as formidable when our hearts and minds are filled with the reality

of God and all He has for us. We are also more prepared to respond enthusiastically to every opportunity God opens to us.

We must understand that the deceiver will deceive us! Very deep, is it not? If someone comes to your door wearing a turban and trying to convert you to Islam, most believers will know better and will not be tempted. But that is not what the enemy does. His distractions come in the form of lusty desires, either toward another person or power, money, position, reputation, and notoriety. He will fill you with envy, anger, hopelessness, jealousy, depression, fear, or a dozen other feelings that will induce self-pity, personal rejection, or loneliness.

Attacks from the enemy are real. He will deliberately calculate what will be the best means to distract you from your destiny, and then he intentionally works out a plan to sidetrack you.

To help us avoid satan's lies, let's remember this parable:

> When an evil spirit comes out of a man, it goes through dry places looking for a place to rest. If the spirit does not find a place, it says, "I will go back to the house from which I came." So, it goes and finds that house empty, cleaned up, and in order. Then the evil spirit goes and brings seven other spirits worse than itself, and they go into that man and live there. And that man has even more trouble than he had before. The evil people of this time will be the same way (Matthew 12:43-45).

It is always quicker to spray fly killer in the house than to look for the nest. But if you take the time to remove the nest, you will never again need the fly spray. Folks will spend a lifetime "spraying" their hearts to rid the flies when something much more basic is needed. Once we finally see the stuff in our hearts that attracts the flies, removal of the stuff will immediately remove the flies as well.

Even a casual look at the Scripture at the beginning of this chapter shows the power of your thoughts and beliefs. No wonder the proverb says, *"Do not eat the bread of a selfish man, or desire his delicacies; for as he thinks within himself, so he is…"* (Prov. 23:6-7 NASB). What you believe is more powerful than you can ever imagine. Your entire life's course is laid out according to what you believe and what you value highly. Think about it. What you believe determines how you pray or *if* you pray. What you believe about forgiveness determines whether or not you believe God will still love you even after you have repeatedly failed. Many are like Peter. After he denied Jesus, he ran away, believing that he did not really love the Lord or that he was unworthy to serve Him any longer. Peter went fishing, left his calling, walked away from his friends—decisions based on his personal beliefs rather than his first-hand knowledge of Jesus. Even though his self-evaluation turned out to be incredibly wrong, he set a new course for his life based on this incorrect understanding of His Lord.

We need to look closer at this Scripture:

> *We live in this world, but we don't fight like people in this world. For our fight we are not using weapons which come from this world. No, our weapons come from God. They are powerful enough to break down strong forts. We break down false logic and anything which rises up against what we know is true about God. We capture every thought to make it obey Christ* (2 Corinthians 10:3-5).

The weapons we fight with have divine power to destroy the fortresses that keep us out of the experience of His Manifest Presence. But what are these fortresses? Are they walls of real stone like the wall around Jericho? Are these walls made of demons that keep us in fear?

According to this incredible Scripture, fortresses are wrong thoughts, doctrines, opinions, prejudices, incorrect theology, and all those things we believe about ourselves that are incorrect. The apostle Paul says that when we destroy speculations as well as every lofty thing that raises itself up against the knowledge of God, we actually take these controlling thoughts captive to the obedience of Jesus Christ. This may sound strange, but I had a personal method of dealing with these negative fortresses and undisciplined thoughts. It was a method that I consciously implemented until I learned to believe what God said about me and my relationship with Him, instead of believing what everyone else said about it.

Even though I personally often fall for it, I don't understand why. After all, I don't let anyone define the love of my wife, Cathy, or our children, so why do I let others define God's love for me? I know deep in my heart what God says about me, feels about me, and wants to do for me. I had to train myself to believe what God says about me. He tells the truth—always.

RECOGNIZE THE LIES

Why does the robber come? Only to steal, kill, and destroy. I came, so that they might have life—to the fullest (John 10:10).

Sometimes the lies of the enemy are so slick that they slip in without even being recognized, but if you are discerning and aware, they are easy to see. God does not speak words that will destroy you. He does not speak negative things that get you depressed and hopeless. His words are words of encouragement, strength, guidance, love, mercy, and hope. Other words are simply not from the Lord.

I mentioned that I had a method, a procedure that helps me bring all my thoughts under His Lordship, obedience to Jesus. When troubling thoughts come to me, I ask myself, "Do these thoughts edify me? Do they strengthen me? Do they try to kill my faith, steal my joy, or destroy my relationship with God or anyone else?"

These are important questions that we must keep in mind. When there is a thought that disturbs my peace in any way, I must analyze the source of these thoughts. When God warns of something, the result is peace, strength, and hope. But when the enemy tells us something unsettling, the result is fear, isolation, and foreboding.

We must learn to pause, ask ourselves these questions calmly. We must be certain that all our thoughts are submitted to the Lordship of Jesus. When our thoughts are lies, they must be stopped. This often means that we must replace the thoughts that are lies with thoughts that are the truth. Merely keeping ourselves busy will give us peace. We keep ourselves engaged emotionally, mentally, and spiritually. This will offer no room for the trickster and give him no time for his lies.

Often the best spiritual warfare is not direct confrontation with the trickster, but knowing who you are so you can simply dismiss his lies.

Check out these powerful words:

> *For though we walk in the flesh, we do not war according to the flesh, for the weapons of our warfare are not of the flesh, but divinely powerful for the destruction of fortresses. We are destroying speculations and every lofty thing raised up against the knowledge of God, and we are taking every thought captive to the obedience of Christ* (2 Corinthians 10:3-5 NASB).

> *For the mind set on the flesh is death, but the mind set on the Spirit is life and peace* (Romans 8:6 NASB).

> *And do not be conformed to this world, but be transformed by the renewing of your mind, that you may prove what the will of God is, that which is good and acceptable and perfect* (Romans 12:2 NASB).

> *I will bless the LORD who has counseled me; Indeed, my mind instructs me in the night* (Psalm 16:7 NASB).

> *The steadfast of mind Thou wilt keep in perfect peace, Because he trusts in You* (Isaiah 26:3 NASB).

> *Set up for yourself roadmarks, Place for yourself guideposts; Direct your mind to the highway, The way by which you*

went. Return, O virgin of Israel, Return to these your cities (Jeremiah 31:21 NASB).

Surely my soul remembers And is bowed down within me. This I recall to my mind, Therefore I have hope. The Lord's lovingkindnesses indeed never cease, For His compassions never fail. They are new every morning; Great is Thy faithfulness. "The Lord is my portion," says my soul, "Therefore I have hope in Him" (Lamentations 3:20-24 NASB).

These negative thoughts are destroyed once and for all through the Truth. The Truth that is in the Book, but also the Truth that is in your heart. Why is Truth capitalized? It is capitalized because the Truth is Jesus Christ Himself who dwells in our hearts by faith, not by works, church attendance, giving, or being good. He, the Truth, dwells within us by faith because He loves us.

The apostle Paul calls some thoughts "lofty." I can just imagine him talking about these lofty, brazen, undisciplined thoughts that lift themselves up against the Truth that is in Jesus. These thoughts separate you from your Lord. These poisonous beliefs keep you weak, confused, and unable to accomplish the things you love to do. They produce guilt, fear, hopelessness, and grief. That is why Paul tells us to submit these thoughts to the Lordship of Jesus (see 2 Cor. 10:5). He will quickly and clearly give us the discernment we need to stand against these poison darts of the liar.

The chances are good that I do not personally know you. But because you are reading this book, there is a good chance that I know your heart. I can sense the hunger, purity, and sincerity of those looking for hope, for answers, and help in their journey to serve the Lord. So I am certain that God is working with you, hoping with you, and giving you all the power and opportunities you need to win in this life. All His resources are available to you. The more you listen to Him, the more you will see what you have never seen and step into experiences that you have never imagined.

NEVER FORGET:
HE ALWAYS TELLS YOU THE TRUTH!

The Lord is my rock, and my fortress, and my deliverer; my God, my strength, in whom I will trust; my buckler, and the horn of my salvation, and my high tower (Psalm 18:2 KJV).

Last of all, be clothed with the Lord Jesus and the power of His strength. Put on all of God's armor. Then you will be able to stand against the evil tricks of the Devil. Our fight is not against human beings. No, it is against rulers, against authorities, against world powers of this darkness, and against evil spiritual beings in the heavenly world. This is why you must take up all of God's armor. Then, when the time for battle comes, you will be able to resist. And, after you have fought your best, you will stand (Ephesians 6:10-13).

He saved me from my powerful enemies, from those who hated me. They were too strong for me (Psalm 18:17).

Nevertheless, I will look to the Always-Present One for help. I will wait confidently for the God of my salvation. My God will listen to me! (Micah 7:7)

I stay close to You. You support me with Your right hand (Psalm 63:8).

APPENDIX

SCRIPTURES THAT WILL HELP YOU OVERCOME THE WORK OF THE TRICKSTER IN YOUR LIFE

You Have Power Over the Enemy

As you study these scriptures, you should understand that the most powerful weapon you have against the trickster is the Word of God. The followings scriptures have the power to destroy the negative work that satan tries to do in you.

These passages should be read prayerfully, meditatively, and faithfully. The word will do its work in you, the believer.

God always stands behind what He says. His Spirit will bring His words into your heart and mind, where true transformation takes place.

> *"And for this reason we also constantly thank God that when you received from us the word of God's message, you accepted it not as the word of men, but for what it really is, the word of God, which also performs its work in you who believe"* (1 Thessalonians 2:13 NASB).

> *Everyone has heard about how you obeyed. I'm proud of you. However, I want you to be wise about good, and simple about evil. The God of peace will crush Satan under your feet*

soon. May the gracious love of Jesus our Lord be with you (Romans 16:19-20).

My little children, you belong to God. You have conquered the false prophets, because the One who is in you is greater than the one who is in the people of the world (1 John 4:4).

This is why I bow down to the Father. Every family in heaven and on earth gets its name from the Father. I pray that God will use His Spirit to give you power from the riches of His glory to make the person inside you strong. Then, through believing in Christ, He will live in your hearts. You will have your roots and foundation in love. Then you and all of the holy people will be able to completely understand the meaning of Christ's love—how wide it is, how long it is, how high it is, and how deep it is. **It goes beyond knowing***, but you will know it. Then you will be filled with the totality of God* (Ephesians 3:14-19).

DISCERNMENT

This is what I am praying for: I want your love to overflow more and more with a fuller knowledge and all insight. Then you will be able to test what is best, so you will be pure and without guilt when Christ comes. You will be filled with what righteousness produces through Jesus Christ for the glory and praise of God (Philippians 1:9-11).

My child, believe what I say. And remember what I command you. Listen to wisdom. Try with all your heart to gain understanding. Cry out for insight. Beg for understanding. Search for it as for silver. Hunt for it like hidden treasure. Then you will understand what it means to revere the Always-Present One. Then you will begin to know God. Only the Always-Present One gives wisdom. Knowledge and understanding come from Him. He stores up a treasure of common sense for those who are honest. Like a shield, He protects those who have integrity. He guards those who are fair to others. He protects those who follow Him. Then you will understand what is honest and fair and right. You will understand what is good to do (Proverbs 2:1-9).

Jesus answered them, "When evening begins, you say, 'It will be good weather tomorrow, because the sky is red.' And, in the morning, you say, 'Today it will be stormy, because the sky is red and dark.' You can understand changes in the sky which show a change in the weather, but you cannot understand the signs of change of this time in history" (Matthew 16:2-3).

HOLDING FAST TO YOUR TESTIMONY

The man answered, "A man called Jesus made some mud and rubbed it on my eyes. Then He told me, 'Go to Siloam and wash yourself.' So I went there and washed myself, and now I can see!" They asked him, "Where is Jesus?" The blind man answered, "I don't know." They brought the man who was once blind to the Pharisees. (Jesus had made the mud and opened the blind man's eyes on the Sabbath day.) Again, the Pharisees kept asking the blind man how he could see. The man said to them, "He put mud on my eyes, I washed myself, and I can see." Some of the Pharisees were saying, "This man is not from God because He does not keep the Sabbath day!" But others were asking, "How could a sinful man perform such miracles?" They were divided among themselves. They asked the man again, "What do you say about Jesus? Do you believe He opened your eyes?" The man answered, "He is a prophet." The Jewish leaders didn't believe that the man had really been blind and could now see, until they called the

*man's parents. The leaders asked them, "Is this man your son?
Do you claim that he was born blind? How come he now
sees?" Then his parents answered, "We know he is our son
and that he was born blind, but we don't know how he can
see now. We don't know how he opened his eyes. Ask him. He
is a grown man; he can speak for himself." (The man's parents said these things, because they were afraid of the Jewish
leaders. The Jewish leaders had already agreed that if anyone
said that Jesus was the Messiah, that person would be thrown
out of the synagogue. That is why his parents said, "He is
an adult; ask him.") Then, a second time, the Jewish leaders
told the man (who had been blind), "Give glory to God! We
know that this man is a sinner." The man answered, "Maybe
He is a sinner. I don't know. But one thing I do know, I was
blind and now I can see"* (John 9:11-25).

COOPERATING WITH GOD

*All people who are being led by God's Spirit are sons of God.
God did not give you a spirit to make you slaves, to be afraid
again. Instead, you received the Spirit who makes you sons.
Through the Spirit, we cry out, "Father, dear Father!" This
same Spirit agrees with our spirits, that we are God's children* (Romans 8:14-16).

*We don't know how we should pray, but the Spirit helps our
weakness. He personally talks to God for us with feelings
which our language cannot express. God searches all men's
hearts. He knows what the Spirit is thinking. The Spirit
talks to God in behalf of holy people, using the manner which
pleases God* (Romans 8:26-27).

*How many people truly understand what is inside just one
person? Only that person's spirit really knows. In the same*

way, only the Spirit of God knows all about God. It is not the spirit of the world which we have received. Instead, we received the Spirit who comes from God, so that we may understand the things which God gave to us. These are the things we are saying. We are not using human ideas of wisdom which man taught us. Instead, we are using words which the Spirit teaches. We explain Spiritual things with Spiritual words. An uninspired person does not receive messages from God's Spirit. To him, they are without meaning; he cannot understand them. They can only be understood in a Spiritual way. The Spiritual person understands everything, but no one completely understands him: "Who can completely understand the Lord's mind? Who can give Him advice?" But **we** *have the mind of Christ!* (1 Corinthians 2:11-16)

The Comforter will teach you everything. He will cause you to remember everything I have told you. He is the Holy Spirit. The Father will send Him with My authority (John 14:26).

Surely you realize that your body is a temple sanctuary? You have received the Holy Spirit from God. The Holy Spirit is inside you—in the temple sanctuary. You don't belong to yourselves (1 Corinthians 6:19).

The healthy words you heard me speak should be kept as an example with the faith and love that is in Christ Jesus. Guard what you were trusted with through the Holy Spirit who lives in us (2 Timothy 1:13-14).

Therefore, be very careful how you live. Don't live like foolish people; live like wise people. Take advantage of every opportunity, because these are evil times. This is why you should not be fools. Instead, try to understand what the Lord wants. Don't get drunk with wine; this leads to wildness.

No, be filled with the Spirit. Use psalms, songs of praise, and spiritual songs to talk to one another. Strum your heart and sing to the Lord (Ephesians 5:15-19).

And, if the Spirit of the One who raised Jesus from death lives in you, then the One who raised Christ from death will make your dead bodies live, using His Spirit who is living in you (Romans 8:11).

You began your life in Christ with the Spirit. Are you trying to continue it by your own power? You are so foolish! Many things have happened to you. Was it all a waste of time? I hope not! Does God give you the Spirit because you follow the law? Does God work miracles among you because you follow the law? It is because you heard the Good News and believed it. The Scriptures say the same thing about Abraham: "Abraham believed God, and so God declared him a righteous man." So, you should know that the true children of Abraham are those who have faith (Galatians 3:3-7).

Listen, You want me to be completely honest. So, teach me true wisdom. Purge me with hyssop, and I will be clean. Wash me; then I will be whiter than snow. Let me hear sounds of joy and gladness. Let the bones that You crushed be happy again. Turn Your face away from my sins. Wipe out all of my guilt! Create a pure heart for me, O God. And renew a solid spirit within me. Do not send me away from Your presence! Don't take Your holy spirit from me. Give me back the joy of Your salvation. Grant me a volunteering attitude to keep me going (Psalm 51:6-12).

RECOGNIZING THE DEVIL'S TRICKS

Then the Spirit led Jesus into the desert to be tempted by the Devil. Jesus did not eat anything for forty days and nights. After this, Jesus was very hungry. The Devil came and said to Jesus, "Since you are the Son of God, command these rocks to become food." Jesus answered, "It is written: 'A person does not live on food alone. Instead, he lives on every word which comes from the mouth of God.'" Then the Devil took Jesus into the holy city, Jerusalem, and put Him on a very high place of the temple. He said to Jesus, "Since You are the Son of God, jump off! Because it is written: 'God will command His angels to take care of You.' And, 'Their hands will catch you, so that you will not hit your foot against a rock.'" Jesus answered him, "But this is also written: 'You must not test the Lord your God.'" Suddenly, the Devil took Jesus to a very tall mountain and showed Him all the kingdoms of the world and the glory which was in them. The Devil said to Jesus, "I will give you all of these things, if You will only bow down to worship me." Then Jesus said to the Devil, "Go away, Satan, because it is written: 'You must worship the Lord your God. Serve only Him.'" Then the Devil left Jesus. Immediately, angels came and helped Him (Matthew 4:1-11).

RECOGNIZING YOUR FLESH

What has been born from men is human. And what has been born from the Spirit is spiritual (John 3:6).

The Spirit is life-giving; physical things are not worth very much. The words I have spoken to you are Spirit and life… (John 6:63).

But if I were to judge, My decision would be right, because I am not alone—the Father who sent Me is with Me, too (John 8:16).

Being Jewish is not just what is on the outside. Circumcision is more than flesh. No, being a Jew depends on what is on the inside. True circumcision is circumcision of the heart performed by the Spirit, not the written code. This person has praise from God, not human beings (Romans 2:28-29).

We know that the law is spiritual, but I am not. I'm human—sold under sin! (Romans 7:14)

People who follow human nature are thinking about the evil things which human nature wants. People who follow the Spirit are thinking about the things that the Spirit wants. The way human nature thinks is death, but the way the Spirit thinks is life and peace. The way human nature thinks is hatred for God. It doesn't want to put itself under the law of God. It can't! People controlled by human nature cannot please God (Romans 8:5-8).

And, if the Spirit of the One who raised Jesus from death lives in you, then the One who raised Christ from death will make your dead bodies live, using His Spirit who is living in you. Therefore, brothers, we shouldn't live by following our human nature. If you do, you will die. If you use the Spirit to kill the evil deeds of the body, you will live. All people who are being led by God's Spirit are sons of God (Romans 8:11-14).

The night is almost gone; daytime is near! So, put away deeds of darkness. Put on the weapons of light. We should live properly, like people do during the daytime, not with orgies or by getting drunk, not committing sexual sin or having wild sex parties, not with fighting or jealousy. Instead, put on the Lord Jesus Christ. Don't think about how to satisfy the evil desires of your human nature (Romans 13:12-14).

Brothers, I couldn't talk to you as I talk to people who are Spiritual. Instead, you were like worldly people, like babies in Christ. I gave you milk to drink, not solid food. You were not yet old enough. Even now you are not ready. You are still worldly. There is jealousy and arguing among you. Are you not worldly then? You are living like sinful people, aren't you? (1 Corinthians 3:1-3)

Surely you realize that your body is a temple sanctuary? You have received the Holy Spirit from God. The Holy Spirit is inside you—in the temple sanctuary. You don't belong to yourselves. You were bought; you cost something. Use your body to give glory to God! (1 Corinthians 6:19-20)

Now we look like the one who came from dust, but we will look like the one who came from heaven. Brothers, I am saying this, because people in their physical form cannot enter the kingdom of God. That which can decay cannot have a share in what never dies (1 Corinthians 15:49-50).

Because of Jesus, those of us who are still alive are always being given up to die. Then the life of Jesus will be made clear in our dying flesh. So, death is active in us, but life is active in you (2 Corinthians 4:11-12).

So, from now on, we really don't know a person by merely looking at his physical body. At one time, we knew about Christ from a human viewpoint, but we do not know Him in that way anymore (2 Corinthians 5:16).

Dear friends, since we have these promises, we should make ourselves clean from anything which might pollute the body or the spirit. Let us be completely holy, showing respect for God (2 Corinthians 7:1).

We live in this world, but we don't fight like people in this world. For our fight we are not using weapons which come from this world. No, our weapons come from God. They are powerful enough to break down strong forts. We break down false logic and anything which rises up against what we know is true about God. We capture every thought to make it obey Christ (2 Corinthians 10:3-5).

So, I tell you: Live by following the Spirit. Then you won't do the selfish and evil things which you want in your human nature. The human nature wants things which are against the Spirit. The Spirit wants things which are against our human nature. These oppose each other. Because of this, you cannot do the things that you really intend to do. But, if you let the Spirit lead you, then you are not under the law. Human nature does things which are wrong. These are clear: committing sexual sin, not being pure, having orgies, worshiping false gods, practicing witchcraft, hating people, making trouble, being jealous, becoming too angry, being selfish, making people angry with each other, causing divisions, envying others, getting drunk, having wild parties, and other such things. I warn you now, as I warned you before: The people who do these things will not inherit God's kingdom. But the Spirit produces: love, joy, peace, patience, kindness, goodness, faithfulness, gentleness, self-control. There is no law against such things as these. Those who belong to Christ Jesus have nailed their own human nature to crosses, along with its feelings and selfish desires. Since we get life from the Spirit, we should follow the Spirit. We must not be conceited or make trouble for each other. Neither should we be jealous of one another (Galatians 5:16-26).

Do not be fooled! You cannot mock God. A person harvests only the things which he plants. If a person lives to satisfy his human nature, then his selfish ways will bring eternal death to him. But, if a person lives to please the Spirit, he will receive eternal life from the Spirit. We must never become tired of doing good. We will receive our harvest of eternal life at the right time. We must never give up! (Galatians 6:7-9)

WHEN I AM WEAK

I've seen some very unusual revelations. God gave me something, so that I would not become too proud—a thorn in the flesh, a messenger of Satan. It always tortures me, stopping me from becoming too proud. I begged the Lord about this three times. I wanted it to go away from me. He said this to me: "My gracious love is enough for you. Power is made perfect in weakness." So I will be very happy to brag about my weaknesses, so that the power of Christ will rest upon me. This is why, for Christ, I can take pleasure in weaknesses, insults, hardships, persecutions, and disasters. Because when I am weak, that's when I am really strong (2 Corinthians 12:7-10).

Of all the apostles, I am the least important. I don't even deserve to be called an apostle; I persecuted the called-out people of God! But I am what I am because of God's gracious love which He pointed toward me. This paid off! I worked harder than all of the other apostles. But, it was not really I that was working so hard—it was God's gracious love which I have with me! (1 Corinthians 15:9-10)

RECOGNIZE NO MAN ACCORDING TO THE FLESH

So, from now on, we really don't know a person by merely looking at his physical body. At one time, we knew about

Christ from a human viewpoint, but we do not know Him in that way anymore. So, if anyone is in Christ, he is a new creation. Old things have passed away. Listen, everything has become new. Everything comes from God. He uses Christ to bring us back to Himself. When God was bringing the people of the world back to Himself in Christ, He was not counting their sins against them. God gave us the message about how He brings people back to Himself. We are representing Christ. It is as though God is encouraging you through us. We beg you, for Christ's sake, come back to God! (2 Corinthians 5:16-20)

HUMANKIND'S NATURE

The entire law is made complete in this one command: "Love other people the same way you love yourself." Be careful! If you continue hurting each other and tearing each other apart, you might completely destroy one another! So, I tell you: Live by following the Spirit. Then you won't do the selfish and evil things which you want in your human nature. The human nature wants things which are against the Spirit. The Spirit wants things which are against our human nature. These oppose each other. Because of this, you cannot do the things that you really intend to do. But, if you let the Spirit lead you, then you are not under the law. Human nature does things which are wrong. These are clear: committing sexual sin, not being pure, having orgies, worshiping false gods, practicing witchcraft, hating people, making trouble, being jealous, becoming too angry, being selfish, making people angry with each other, causing divisions, envying others, getting drunk, having wild parties, and other such things. I warn you now, as I warned you before: The people who do these things will not inherit God's kingdom. But the Spirit produces: love, joy, peace, patience, kindness, goodness, faith-fulness, gentleness, self-control. There is no law against such things as these. Those who belong to Christ Jesus have nailed their own human nature to crosses, along with its feelings and selfish desires. Since we get life from the Spirit, we should follow the Spirit. We must not be conceited or make trouble for each other. Neither should we be jealous of one another (Galatians 5:14-26).

So, there is no condemnation now for those people who are in Christ Jesus. The law of the Spirit of life in Christ Jesus has set me free from the law of sin and death. The law was weak through human nature. God did what the law couldn't do: He sent His own Son as an offering for sin. He came with a nature like man's sinful human nature. And concerning sin, this is how God used human nature to condemn sin. He wanted to completely satisfy in us what the law says is right. We are living by following the Spirit, not by follow-ing human nature. People who follow human nature are thinking about the evil things which human nature wants. People who follow the Spirit are thinking about the things that the Spirit wants. The way human nature thinks is death, but the way the Spirit thinks is life and peace. The way human nature thinks is hatred for God. It doesn't want to put itself under the law of God. It can't! People controlled by human nature cannot please God. However, you are not being controlled by human nature; you are being controlled by the Spirit—if God's Spirit lives in you. If anyone does not have Christ's Spirit, this person does not belong to Christ. But since Christ is in you, even though your body is dying (because of sin), your spirit is alive (because you have been made right with God). And, if the Spirit of the One who raised Jesus from death lives in you, then the One who raised Christ from death will make your dead bodies live, using His

Spirit who is living in you. Therefore, brothers, we shouldn't live by following our human nature. If you do, you will die. If you use the Spirit to kill the evil deeds of the body, you will live. All people who are being led by God's Spirit are sons of God. God did not give you a spirit to make you slaves, to be afraid again. Instead, you received the Spirit who makes you sons. Through the Spirit, we cry out, "Father, dear Father!" This same Spirit agrees with our spirits, that we are God's children. Since we are children, we are also heirs—heirs of God and co-heirs with Christ. If we suffer together, we will share glory together (Romans 8:1-17).

WHO HAS SEEN THE LORD?

The heavens declare the glory of God; the skies proclaim the work of His hands. Day after day they pour forth speech; night after night they display knowledge. There is no speech or language where their voice is not heard (Psalm 19:1-3 NIV).

WORLD CHANGERS SEE THE LORD

Isaiah

In the year that King Uzziah died, I saw the Lord seated on a throne, high and exalted, and the train of His robe filled the temple. Above Him were seraphs, each with six wings: With two wings they covered their faces, with two they covered their feet, and with two they were flying. And they were calling to one another: "Holy, holy, holy is the Lord Almighty; the whole earth is full of His glory." At the sound of their voices the doorposts and thresholds shook and the temple was filled with smoke. "Woe to me!" I cried. "I am ruined! For I am a man of unclean lips, and I live among a people of unclean lips, and my eyes have seen the King, the Lord Almighty." Then one of the seraphs flew to me with a live coal in his hand, which he had taken with tongs from the altar. With it he touched my mouth and said, "See, this has touched your lips; your guilt is taken away and your sin atoned for." Then I heard the voice of the Lord saying, "Whom shall I send? And who will go for Us?" And I said, "Here am I. Send me!" He said, "Go and tell this people: 'Be ever hearing, but never understanding; be ever seeing, but never perceiving" (Isaiah 6:1-9 NIV).

David

David said about Him: "'I saw the Lord always before me. Because he is at my right hand, I will not be shaken. Therefore my heart is glad and my tongue rejoices; my body also will live in hope, because you will not abandon me to the grave, nor will you let Your Holy One see decay. You have made known to me the paths of life; you will fill me with joy in your presence" (Acts 2:25-28 NIV).

Paul

I knew a man in Christ fourteen years ago. This man was caught up to the third heaven. I don't know whether he was in his physical body or not—God knows. But I know such a person. Again, I don't know if he was in or out of his physical body—God knows. This man was caught up to Paradise. He heard things which cannot be re-told; a man is not allowed to tell such things to other men (2 Corinthians 12:2-4).

John

That which was from the beginning, which we have heard, which we have seen with our eyes, which we have looked at and our hands have touched—this we proclaim concerning the Word of life. The life appeared; we have seen it and testify to it, and we proclaim to you the eternal life, which was with the Father and has appeared to us. We proclaim to you what we have seen and heard, so that you also may have fellowship with us. And our fellowship is with the Father and with His Son, Jesus Christ (1 John 1:1-3 NIV).

MEDITATION

Now there was a certain disciple at Damascus, named Ananias; and the Lord said to him in a vision, "Ananias." And he said, "Behold, here am I, Lord."

And the Lord said to him, "Arise and go to the street called Straight, and inquire at the house of Judas for a man from Tarsus named Saul, for behold, he is praying,

and he has seen in a vision a man named Ananias come in and lay his hands on him, so that he might regain his sight" (Acts 9:10-12 NASB).

And on the next day, as they were on their way, and approaching the city, Peter went up on the housetop about the sixth hour to pray.

And he became hungry, and was desiring to eat; but while they were making preparations, he fell into a trance;

and he beheld the sky opened up, and a certain object like a great sheet coming down, lowered by four corners to the ground, and there were in it all kinds of four-footed animals and crawling creatures of the earth and birds of the air.

And a voice came to him, "Arise, Peter, kill and eat!"

But Peter said, "By no means, Lord, for I have never eaten anything unholy and unclean."

And again a voice came to him a second time, "What God has cleansed, no longer consider unholy."

And this happened three times; and immediately the object was taken up into the sky (Acts 10:9-16 NASB).

"I was in the city of Joppa praying; and in a trance I saw a vision, a certain object coming down like a great sheet lowered by four corners from the sky; and it came right down to me,

and when I had fixed my gaze upon it and was observing it I saw the four-footed animals of the earth and the wild beasts and the crawling creatures and the birds of the air.

"And I also heard a voice saying to me, 'Arise, Peter; kill and eat.

"But I said, 'By no means, Lord, for nothing unholy or unclean has ever entered my mouth.'

"But a voice from heaven answered a second time, 'What God has cleansed, no longer consider unholy.'

"And this happened three times, and everything was drawn back up into the sky.

"And behold, at that moment three men appeared before the house in which we were staying, having been sent to me from Caesarea.

"And the Spirit told me to go with them without misgivings. And these six brethren also went with me, and we entered the man's house.

"And he reported to us how he had seen the angel standing in his house, and saying, 'Send to Joppa, and have Simon, who is also called Peter, brought here

and he shall speak words to you by which you will be saved, you and all your household' (Acts 11:5-14 NASB).

ABOUT THE AUTHOR

D ON NORI SR. is the founder of Destiny Image Publishers and MercyPlace Ministries. MercyPlace Ministries is a non-profit renewal and revival ministry whose focus is to bring Jesus to a world that desperately needs Him.

DON NORI, SR. • FOUNDER, DESTINY IMAGE

www.donnorisr.com

MINISTRY PAGE

If you would like to order copies of this book or messages preached by Don Nori Sr. visit:

www.destinyimage.com

If you would like to contact Don Nori Sr. regarding a speaking engagement, please e-mail him at publisher@destinyimage.com or contact his assistant,

Alex Sadowski at 717-532-3040 ext. 124

Additional copies of this book and other
book titles from DESTINY IMAGE are
available at your local bookstore.

Call toll-free: 1-800-722-6774.

Send a request for a catalog to:

Destiny Image® Publishers, Inc.

P.O. Box 310
Shippensburg, PA 17257-0310

*"Speaking to the Purposes of God for This
Generation and for the Generations to Come."*

For a complete list of our titles,
visit us at www.destinyimage.com.